# MOTO GUZZI

Illustrated

# MOTO GUZZI
## BUYER'S ★ GUIDE ™

## Mick Walker

**Aston Publications**

Sole distributors for the USA

*Motorbooks International*
Publishers & Wholesalers Inc.

Published in 1992 by Aston Publications Limited
Bourne End House, Harvest Hill
Bourne End, Bucks, SL8 5JJ

The information in this book is true and complete
to the best of our knowledge. All
recommendations are made without any
guarantee on the part of the author or the
publisher, who also disclaim any liability incurred
in connection with the use of this data or specific
details.

We recognise that some words, model names and
designations, for example, mentioned herein are
the property of the trademark holder. We use
them for identification purposes only. This is not
an official publication.

ISBN 0 946627 74 6

Designed by Chris Hand

Printed in Hong Kong

Sole distributors in the UK
Springfield Books Limited
Norman Road, Denby Dale
Huddersfield, West Yorkshire HD8 8TH

Sole distributors in the United States
Motorbooks International
P.O. Box 2
729 Prospect Avenue, Osceola
Wisconsin 54020
United States

# Acknowledgements

Moto Guzzi is one of the most famous of all Italian motorcycle marques and, with Gilera and MV Agusta, one of the 'Big Three' which achieved lasting fame for their racing exploits over many years.

Guzzi owners are also a somewhat special breed. Virtually every one of them is in the enthusiast category – real motorcyclists. So this book is something special too, its potential readership being like-minded souls to myself.

My personal experience with Moto Guzzi comes both from ownership of several models down through the years, and to being a Guzzi dealer for almost a decade, acting as the British spares importer for the marque and finally road testing a host of them during my spell of journalism with *Motorcycle Enthusiast* magazine between 1983 and 1989.

During this period I have been lucky enough to build up a number of friends who are involved with Guzzis in some way, whether it be at factory level, as British importers, or simply loyal riders of the marque. Without these good people this book would have been much more difficult to compile.

The following list is not in any order of merit, but simply as they came to mind – all were helpful in some way. If I've missed anyone I can but apologise, it was not my intention.

At the Mandello del Lario factory, both Guido Rinalli and Gemma Pedretta gave their full support to the project and provided information and photographs. I was also given full access to all Guzzi's facilities, including the Museum.

In Britain the UK distributors, Three Cross Imports Ltd., were not only helpful but their enthusiasm is genuine for the product they are selling. Special thanks go to Keith Davies, Mike Shorten and Tina Hicks for giving 100 per cent support whilst I was compiling the *Illustrated Moto Guzzi Buyers Guide*.

The Moto Guzzi Club GB, through the General Secretary, Simon Howers, helped by providing information not only on their organization, but Guzzi in general.

Two Australian long-term Guzzi owners deserve special praise – Jim Heaven and Keith McKenhnie – thanks a million, guys.

I also received assistance from Bernard Adey (Spares GB), Amede Castellani, Fran Contaldi (Moto America), Gary Cotterell (Denver Garage), Hoss Elm (Moto Cinelli), Greg Field, Doug Jackson, Rick Kemp, Erhard Lienke, Vincent Marcello, Richard Walker and Arthur Wheeler.

The vast majority of photographs came either from the factory archives or my own collection. However, valuable input in this area was also received from Doug Jackson, the late Don Upshaw and Richard Walker, amongst others.

My thanks also go to my secretary, Kim White, for typing the manuscript.

Finally, to Anthony Pritchard of Aston Publications for approaching me with the original idea.

I hope the result makes interesting reading and, at the same time, that it will assist existing and potential owners alike in answering some of the many questions that usually remain hidden from general view.

I am sure that if you get half as much fun and enjoyment from being involved with Moto Guzzi as I have then you will be happy.

Mick Walker
Wisbech, Cambridgeshire
December 1991

# How To Use This Book

This is not intended to be yet another book on the history of motorcycling, or one of particular technical details, rather it is to help the owner, restorer, potential buyer or simply a committed enthusiast for Moto Guzzi motorcycles to avoid a few of the pitfalls which might catch out the unwary. But most of all the intention is to provide a general guide on just what bikes are the most sought after – collectable – of the many models produced by the famous Italian marque since their entry into the motorcycle arena in the early 1920s.

Like the stock market, whether you collect, restore or just use a motorcycle, it can go up or down in value and nobody, myself included, has all the answers. So you should become involved with Moto Guzzi through genuine enthusiasm not simply as a financial investment for the future.

### Prices

To simplify matters all prices quoted are approximate. For readers with different currencies a simple conversion will reveal the value. However, with currency fluctuations this can only be a rough guide and should *not* be taken as the exact price. In any case prices are constantly changing, so the best system is to study the various national and local press publications before starting your search.

### Rating system

★      A model which has not received particular attention or enthusiasm from potential owners in the past. Usually readily available – whether produced originally in small or large numbers.

May have potential in the future, and has the advantage of the lowest current price. Conversely the majority of machines in this category will remain largely unwanted.

★★      In this category come the motorcycles which proved popular when new, are still in widespread use and *may* in future, when fewer are around, appreciate in buyer/collector interest

and therefore value. But you are taking a risk as an investment.

★★★      This is the average, one which should hold its value, but you are never going to make a fortune out of it. Offers its owner considerable enjoyment out on the open road. Buy for use rather than investment.

★★★★      Valuable now – and in the future. But because of its desirability will already be expensive. It will continue to rise in future, but just how much is uncertain.

★★★★★      The real classic. If you find one at a realistic price snap it up now, it's going to become a special bike that even more people will want in the future, meaning that its value will go up faster than machines in the other star ratings.

### Important note

Prices are *greatly* influenced by condition, serviceability and originality – but no guide can make up for the experienced eye, so if you do not feel you come into this category make sure you find someone who does and take him along before parting with your money. Work needed to be done, including parts, should be deducted from estimated values.

However much you may feel you need the bike, it is best to be patient. By adopting this method you are less likely to suffer heartache.

I have attempted, by writing this book, to help Moto Guzzi buyers find a good bike at a fair price. Most Guzzi owners are experienced enthusiasts who share a mutual respect and interest in the product. But don't accept this to be the case every time around, size up each individual seller independently. It's much better to be safe than sorry.

Finally specials, whether home built, or professionally constructed, are generally of considerably less value than (original) standard production models of the same vintage. This is because they reflect one man's dream, rather than a concept which will appeal to a wider audience.

# Contents

# CHAPTER 1

# Setting the Scene

The unlikely setting of squadron life in the Italian Air Service during the latter stages of the Great War in 1918 was instrumental in the creation of what is now regarded by many as that nation's most famous motorcycle marque, Moto Guzzi.

Two pilots, Giovanni Ravelli and Giorgio Parodi, together with Carlo Guzzi, their young mechanic/driver, talked of little else than an advanced design of motorcycle, which Guzzi had sketched out in off-duty hours.

Sadly, Ravelli was doomed never to see Guzzi's handiwork reach fruition, as he lost his life on a flying mission shortly after the end of hostilities in September 1918. But both Giorgio Parodi and Carlo Guzzi came through the war unscathed and quickly decided to press on with their wartime dream of their own brand of motorcycle.

The pair's major problem was finance, or, more accurately the lack of it, but luckily Parodi came from a wealthy family; his father, Emanuele, was the owner of a prosperous shipping line based at Genoa. And it was Parodi Senior who provided the loan which set the fledgling partnership on its way in January 1919 (a copy of the original three page agreement can be seen in the Guzzi museum).

With adequate finance in place and the design drawn up in detail, the time had come to transform the dream into reality. The first prototype was given the name GP (for Guzzi-Parodi), but by the time the magazine *Motociclisimo* announced the new marque publicly for the first time in December 1920, the name had been changed to the familiar Moto Guzzi. Not only this, but the fledgling company had adopted a new trademark, an eagle with its wings spread in flight. The emblem, proudly borne by Guzzi motorcycles to this day, was chosen by Guzzi and Parodi to commemorate their fallen comrade Giovanni Ravelli, and the air service in which they had all served.

For its time, the prototype was a revolutionary design. Its 498cc single-cylinder engine was laid horizontally and featured overhead cam driven by shaft and bevel gears. Perhaps even more interesting were the four-valve head layout and the engine's oversquare (short-stroke) dimensions of 88×82mm bore and stroke.

The first production models closely followed the original layout, but the overhead cam was changed to overhead valve operation, and the machine employed a more conventional two-valve cylinder head.

The new company's ten employees built 17 motorcycles that first year (1921), but the design, with its giant outside flywheel, semi-unit construction gearbox, and magneto ignition mounted centrally above the engine/gearbox was to remain in production,

The very first production Moto Guzzi was the Normale of 1921. Its inlet-over-exhaust horizontal engine had a capacity of 498.4cc.

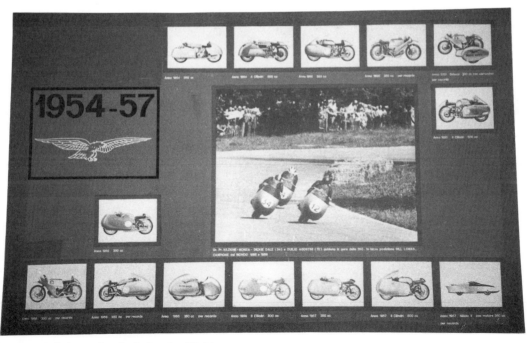

Montage of photographs displaying the 'Golden Era' of Guzzi racing, from 1954 till their retirement from GP racing at the end of 1957.

A line of Guzzis in the factory's museum. It has been a tradition to retain one of each model down through the years. Recently a factory official commented, 'The museum is now worth more than the works itself!'

Police and military contracts have long been a major source of revenue for the Mandello del Lario company. This photograph shows a Milan-based *policewoman* in late 1985 with her 850 T3 Polizia model.

albeit updated from time to time, until as late as 1976 – still retaining its original 88×82mm engine dimensions.

Over the years, many variations of the classic format appeared, including Tipo GT, Tipo Sport, GT16, Sport 14 and 15, V, GTV, GTW, GTC, S, GTS, the Condor and Dondolino clubman's racers, Astore – and finally, perhaps the best known of all – the Falcone.

Apart from this wide selection of '500s', the flat-single layout was also manufactured in other capacities. The first was the 175cc P175 of 1932, followed by a derivative of 238cc, the P250. Production of both these models ceased with Italy's entry into the Second World War in June 1940, but in any case, an improved 250, the Airone had made its début in 1939, and this model remained in production until as late as 1957. The Airone, with a 247cc engine, was available in touring or sports guise, and was an extremely popular model in the boom days of post-war Italy.

Right from the start Moto Guzzi realized the importance of racing as an effective means of publicity, and they were active in this branch of the sport until their final withdrawal at the end of the 1957 season. During their racing years Guzzi made a significant contribution to the glamour and excitement of motorcycle racing and were one of the most successful marques, with a string of World Championship and TT victories to their credit.

The Mandello concern will always be remembered for their amazing versatility in racing design, for, in addition to the famous singles, they produced machines with V-twin, across-the-frame 3, in-line 4, and V8 engines. Guzzi also built a special wind tunnel to test and develop streamlining for their machines which contributed enormously to their racing and record-breaking success. The roll of famous riders that achieved major acclaim on Guzzi machinery is an impressive one, including Stanley Woods, Omobono Tenni, Fergus Anderson, Maurice Cann, Bruno Ruffo, Enrico Lorenzetti, Dickie Dale, Ken Kavanagh, Bill Lomas and Keith Campbell.

Of all the racing designs mentioned above,

The Mandello del Lario factory photographed in the late 1930's.

The current Moto Guzzi Export Manager, Guido Rinalli, at his desk in November 1988.

the one that achieved the most was a direct descendant of the very first Guzzi – the horizontal single (but of 350cc) – that scored an impressive five successive World Championship titles, beating the best 4-cylinder designs which MV Agusta and Gilera could throw against it.

On the production side, following the Second World War, Guzzi reinforced its position as the largest of all Italy's motorcycle manufacturers with a range which not only included the ever popular horizontal four-stroke singles, but a new series of small capacity two-strokes and an interesting motorcycle-cum-scooter called the Galletto.

Other popular post-war singles – both four-strokes, were the Lodola and Stornello, but towering above all these is the long-running range of 90-degree V-twins, which began with the original 700cc V7 in the mid-1960s and continue in various engine capacities between 350 and 1000cc today.

# CHAPTER 2

# Strokers

| | | |
|---|---|---|
| ** | Guzzino 65 | 1946-54 |
| ** | Cardellino | 1953-65 |
| ** | Zigolo | 1953-66 |
| ' | 125 Turismo and Tuttoterreno | |
| * | All other models | 1974-81 |

**History**

Prior to the end of the Second World War, the Moto Guzzi company had no experience whatsoever of manufacturing or selling two-stroke motorcycles. However, this didn't stop the Mandello del Lario engineers from developing a whole series of such models during the post-war era.

This decision was taken for the soundest of commercial reasons. Pre-war, the motorcycle had never, for the most part, been viewed in Italy as anything other than a sporting vehicle for the diehard enthusiast, but with the cessation of hostilities, with the four-wheel fleet almost annihilated, public transport in disarray, and fuel and raw materials at a premium, the lightweight motorcycle appeared (and was largely accepted) to be the answer to the population's need for mobility.

Some of the machines were basic in the extreme, some were expensive but unreliable, some manufacturers saw the answer in the micromotor-assisted bicycle, whilst yet more thought the scooter to be the best answer.

But of course Guzzi, with their traditional leading position within the Italian motorcycle industry, opted for another solution: a high-quality lightweight powered by an extremely efficient rotary-valve two-stroke engine. The result was the Guzzino (little Guzzi).

**Guzzino 65**

The '65' was designed by Ing. Antonio Micucci, who had joined Guzzi in the winter of 1942. He was appointed Managing Designer in 1945 and the new two-stroke was his first design in this post.

The rotary-valve engine had a capacity of 64cc (42×46mm). Running on a low 5.5:1 compression ratio because of the low octane fuel then available, it produced a modest 2 bhp at 5000 rpm, which provided a maximum speed just in excess of 30 mph, a figure that could be achieved almost regardless of load. But its real forté was excellent fuel consumption and it usually averaged an impressive 150-200 mpg.

The cylinder head and barrel were both cast in light alloy and the barrel featured a cast-iron liner. Lubrication was provided by petrol/oil mixture at a ratio of 20:1. Carburation was taken care of by a Dell'Orto MA13 instrument.

The transmission consisted of helical-geared primary drive, a wet multi-plate clutch and a 3-speed hand-operated gearbox, the lever of which was mounted on the offside of the 6.5-litre fuel tank. Final drive was via a ½ by $\frac{3}{16}$ in chain.

Few changes were made to the tiny machine's specification during its production life except for a horn and modified silencer tail pipe in 1948; a strengthened rear fork in 1949; and a move to a cast-iron barrel in 1953.

The first Guzzi two-stroke was this tiny 64cc Guzzino. It sold in large numbers between 1946 and 1954.

An interesting aftermarket conversion was a kit offered by a Bergamese concern which transformed the Guzzino into a 73cc *four-stroke,* complete with fully enclosed valves, and a lubrication system made up of a gear-type feed and return pump.

The tiny Guzzi sold in larger numbers than any other Italian motorcycle of the immediate post-war era, and over 200,000 were produced between 1946 and 1954.

### Cardellino

The Cardellino (Goldfinch) was essentially a renamed Guzzino when it first appeared at the end of 1953. Like the final Guzzino it used a cast-iron cylinder barrel, but with a larger Dell'Orto MU14 B2 carburettor. The rest of the machine remained unchanged, with the exception of 20in rather than 26in wheels, and a redesigned rear frame. The latter was the result of the often vast loads of passengers and goods which owners had subjected the tiny Guzzi two-stroke to in the past.

The first real changes to the specification came in 1956, when early that year the

Cardellino gained a pair of undamped telescopic forks, replacing the original blade-type, which had also been a feature of the Guzzino since it entered production a decade earlier. The mudguards were also replaced by a new design which gave more comprehensive protection, and full-width alloy brake drums were fitted.

Later the same year, at the Milan Show, a larger capacity variant was announced known as the '73'. This name reflected its engine capacity, which had been increased by adding 3mm to the bore (45mm). Other improvements were an increase in maximum power (up to 2.6 bhp) and the replacement of the tank-mounted hand gearchange to a foot-operated lever.

Two years on, at the 1958 Milan Show, the Nuovo (New) Cardellino was launched. Although if retained the 73cc engine, the cylinder barrel was now of the flash-chromed alloy variety. This was fine for closer tolerances and improved ring sealing, but a real pig if the bore became damaged, as the only remedy was a new cylinder assembly.

BILL LOMAS,
WERELDKAMPIOEN 1956
OP 350 CC MOTO GUZZI

# MOTO GUZZI
*,,Zigolo''*

Dutch brochure for the 98cc Zigolo series 1, making use of the Italian factory's racing heritage.

This model remained in production unchanged until superseded by the definitive version, the '83', which made its first public appearance at Milan in November 1962 and stayed in production until 1965.

## Zigolo

The Zigolo (Bunting) largely took over from where the best-selling Guzzino '65' left off. It was launched at the Milan Spring Fair in April 1953 and for its day brought an air of luxury to the previously unexciting ultralight class. Far from being purely a bigger bore Guzzino, the vast majority of the newcomer's specification was brand new, and once again was the work of Ing. Micucci.

Although the engine was still of the rotary-valve type, it now featured a totally horizontal cylinder, with the Dell'Orto MAF 15B1 carb mounted on the other side to that of the smaller unit. With square engine dimensions, the 50 × 50mm bore and stroke provided a capacity of exactly 98cc. Running on a compression ratio of 6:1, its 4 bhp provided road speeds of, 18, 28 and 47 mph through the three-speed box.

It used a pressed-steel chassis, with partial enclosure. In the suspension department, the Zigolo was provided with a pair of undamped telescopic front forks and rear springing by a rubber element in compression with friction-type damping. Another change was the use of smaller diameter 19in wheels, and 2.50 section tyres.

For the 1954 model year, a Lusso (de luxe) version was offered for sale alongside the standard bike. This differed in its specification, with a dual seat, 17in tyres and a new colour scheme. The standard 98 Zigolo was finished in grey, whereas the Lusso was painted in the much more striking Italian racing red. In addition the tank sides were chrome-plated.

A Zigolo Lusso was tested by *Motor Cycling* in their 29 September, 1955, issue and they recorded 51 mph, which at least proved that Guzzi, unlike many manufacturers, were not ones to make excessive performance claims that could not be met out on the open road. This was no ordinary test either, as the tiny Guzzi was subjected to over 3000 miles in the hands of the magazine's testers. So it proved

Zigolo engine, showing carburettor installation (rotary valve induction), horizontal cylinder layout and kickstarter mechanism.

to be as much an assessment of the Zigolo's durability at its performance capabilities. From this searching test the Guzzi 'emerged with flying colours' and in the process not only proved itself a reliable lightweight but also the fastest machine under 100cc tested by *Motor Cycling* up to that time.

The Zigolo's engine came in for particular praise. 'Almost completely vibrationless, it would rev beautifully and yet pull like a steam engine on hills. Top gear could be held down to 10 mph, enabling hills with single-figure gradients to be ascended without cog-swapping.'

A mildly tuned version the Zigolo Sport appeared in 1954. This was essentially identical to the Lusso, but with a power output of 6.8 bhp. To confuse the issue, at the same time the standard 'cooking' model

Various versions of the 48.9cc (38.5×42mm) Dingo ultra-lightweight motorcycle. Left to right: GT, Super and Cross. Circa 1967.

MOTO GUZZI

trotter 40cc

The last design
undertaken by Ing.
Antonio Micucci was the
40cc Trotter, with two-
speed automatic gearbox.

became the Turismo, with only very slight cosmetic differences (for example, the front section of the tank was finished in black).

From the 1958 season Guzzi offered the 98 Zigolo Series II. Together with the Cardellino, the new Zigolo was the first Italian series production motorcycle to employ an alloy cylinder *without* the conventional cast-iron liner. Instead, a layer of hard chrome-plating was applied directly to the alloy using a unique electrolytic process pioneered in Germany.

In theory the benefits were considerable. Not only was cooling more efficient, but the

# MOTO GUZZI

Why Moto-Guzzi have the flying eagle above their name?

Just after the first world war two young and enthusiastic aviators by the names of Carlo Guzzi and Giorgio Parodi set about building a new kind of Motor Cycle.

The first machine to emerge from their small workshop in Mandello del Lario was a horizontal single cylinder 4-stroke of 500 cc.

Rather romantically to encourage the machine to fly they painted a flying eagle on the tank, and entered the machine in the famous Targa Florio Race.

The machine won, and this successful machine complete with the flying eagle was put into full production.

The following year Moto-Guzzi was operational. New advanced 4-stroke machines were successfully developed over the following years, exciting machines breaking new grounds in engine technology many capable of 100 M.P.H. All these machines handled superbly.

By 1930 Moto-Guzzi built their first 4-cylinder machine – a water cooled 4-stroke (see the Japanese were not first).

The continued success of their production machines eventually brought about their participation in Grand Prix Racing, and they were to dominate the 250cc and 350cc classes from 1948 to 1957, winning a total of nine world championships during this period. 1955 saw the birth of probably the most exciting Motor Cycle ever produced, the fabulous 500 cc V-8 cylinder Grand Prix Racer which was tested at 185 M.P.H. over 20 years ago.

So the story of this famous market continues. In 1975 they introduced the revolutionary Integral Safety Brake System to Motor Cycles (patented), and put into production the first Motor Cycle with automatic transmission.

Over 50 years later the eagle is still flying proudly above the Moto-Guzzi name.

**CHIÜ**
49 cc 2-STROKE

**CROSS 50**
49 cc 2-STROKE

**125 TURISMO**
125 cc 1 CYLINDER
2-STROKE

**125 TUTTOTERRENO**

**250 TS**
2 CYLINDERS 2-STROKE

Two-stroke models from the 1980 Moto Guzzi range. Top to bottom: Chiu, Cross, Turismo, Tuttoterreno and 250TS. All were badge-engineered Benelli-based bikes.

A modern Guzzi stroker. The 125 Custom
introduced at the Milan Show in November 1985. It
was not imported into Britain.

engine could employ reduced piston-to-bore
clearances and still need *less* lubrication. In
fact, the amount of oil could be reduced to
around 50:1 (compared to 20:1 for the
conventional Zigolo engine), resulting in
improved overall performance. The factory
quoted 131 mpg at two-thirds throttle on
level roads, or 100 mpg full bore (both figures
proving remarkably accurate).

All this was fine provided (as already
mentioned in the Cardellino section) that
you did not need to replace the barrel.
However, in fairness, the system did work
and replacement barrels were the exception
rather than the norm (unlike certain other
Italian two-strokes that employed this
system during the 1970s).

The Series II also differed in the following
respects: full-width brake hubs, a
redesigned cylinder head, improvements to
the rotary valve system, 17in tyres, modified
front forks and revised cosmetics.

The final version of the Zigolo was the
'110', which was offered from 1960 to 1966.
This superseded the '98' totally, the last of
which were manufactured in late 1959. The
larger capacity of 110.3cc was achieved by
increases in both the bore and stroke by
2mm: 52×52mm. At the same time the
compression ratio was upped to 7.5:1 to take
best advantage of the improved octane fuel
which was by then widely available. There
was also a larger Dell'Orto MAF 18B1
carburettor. But in other respects the basic

engine specification remained as before.

With 4.8 bhp on tap the '110' was hardly any more powerful than its predecessor, although the torque figures had been usefully increased to provide better low-speed performance. The 3-speed gearbox remained, but with a modified clutch. A car-type 'box' silencer replaced the original conventional motorcycle one found on the '98'.

It was in the cycle parts where the real differences were to be found. Most important of these was the suspension system, notably the improved front forks, which now featured hydraulic damping. Another major improvement in this area was the new swinging arm with twin hydraulically controlled dampers.

The *Motor Cycle* tested the '110' Zigolo in early 1964 and found the maximum speed to be 55 mph and had this to say; 'Easy on the eye, fun to ride, yet not a bank-breaker when it comes to sordid finance'.

## Others

These range from the Dingo and Trotter 50cc models of the late 1960s and early 1970s to the Benelli-based 250 TS parallel twin manufactured from 1974 until 1982. Most were basically reliable if unexciting performers. But models definitely to stay well clear of are the single-cylinder piston-port 125 Turismo and Tuttoterreno models (1974-1981). Both of these were cheaply constructed and depressingly unreliable.

## What to look for

None of the Guzzi two-strokes are really collectable. However, the early rotary valve models such as the '65' and Zingolo are the best of the bunch – but spares are difficult, if not impossible, to find. The models from the 1970s and 1980s are generally less than perfect and in any case are essentially badge-engineered Benellis, although spares are easier to find.

## Star Ratings

Guzzino 65, Cardellino and Zigolo two stars, others one star – except the 125 Turismo and Tuttoterreno, which hardly deserve a feeble half star.

# CHAPTER 3

# Gentleman racers

| | | |
|---|---|---|
| **** | **GTC** | **1937-39** |
| ***** | **Condor** | **1938-40** |
| ***** | **Dondolino** | **1946-51** |
| ***** | **Gambalunga** | **1946-51** |

## History

This breed of ultra-sporting Guzzi single could trace its history back to the mid-1930s, when with racing at factory level becoming increasingly popular, there was a growing demand for over-the-counter racers, machines which the ordinary man in the street could afford. In Italy, several manufacturers responded to the needs of this market and the era of 'Gentleman racers' was born.

The bikes were supposed to be production racers sold with a full set of road accessories, including lighting equipment, kickstarter and silencer. Although the concept was well intentioned, in their bid for glory the majority of manufacturers soon began to produce machines that were little different from full works racers except for a light camouflage of road equipment.

This led to another problem in that, instead of providing sport for everyone as had been the original idea, the prices of these highly tuned specialist machines put them out of the reach of all but the very well-heeled. In other words, hardly any aspiring production race riders could afford to buy a production bike.

## GTC

Guzzi meanwhile had gone about things in its own particular fashion. Initially, they responded to the demand by producing the GTC – little more than a souped-up version of the standard GTW sports roadster (see Chapter 2). Although this was reliable enough, the GTC was neither sufficiently fast nor its handling adequate to compete successfully as a racer.

It was, however, in many ways an excellent clubman's type of machine in the fashion of the later BSA Gold Star. But at the time of its production in 1937, the GTC was ajudged a failure for its intended purpose, and that was what mattered. This prompted the Mandello del Lario factory to build something different, something more in tune with the racetrack than with the street.

## Condor

The result was the *Nouvo C* (New C), which soon became known as the Condor. Although it retained the general Guzzi flat-single ohv configuration, including the same 88×82mm bore and stroke measurements, the Condor was largely a new machine.

The cylinder head and barrel were of alloy instead of cast iron, there was a single exhaust pipe and silencer, 32mm Dell'Orto SS racing carburettor, and a set of close-ratio gears selected by a typically Italian heel-and-toe pedal.

When launched in 1938, the asking price was 11,000 lire (which at the conversion rate of the period made it around the same price as an International Norton). For that the

Second of Guzzi's 'Gentleman racers', the 500 Condor Sport of 1938, shown here with all road-going equipment.

A 1939 Condor in full racing trim. Note the traditional Guzzi features such as the horizontal engine, the massive 'bacon slicer' outside flywheel and the tank-top oil container.

buyer obtained a power output of 28 bhp at 5000 rpm, sufficient to propel the 498.4cc Condor to a maximum speed of 100 mph.

Part of the secret of its speed was the frame, which was entirely new, with the rear section constructed from Hydronalium, a special lightweight alloy of great strength which was widely used within the aviation industry.

Other features included 21in alloy rims and 220mm brakes front and rear. Like the crankcases, the hubs and brake plates were cast in elektron-magnesium alloy. This attention to weight saving added up to a total package weighing only 140kg, some 20kg lower than the GTC.

For road use the Condor came complete with a dynamo (located over the crankcase behind the magneto), left-hand kickstarter and centre-stand. By removing these, the weight could be reduced by a further 15kg.

An 18-litre fuel tank with a separate 3.5-litre oil container carried over it gave the machine an almost pioneer style. But with a fuel consumption under racing conditions of around 45mpg, the Condor was capable of covering longer distances between stops than the vast majority of its competitors.

Guzzi's new 'Gentleman racer' got off to a resounding start very soon after its launch by winning the prestigious local Lario circuit classic of 1938. The following year, the final staging of the event (known as Italy's TT), saw future World Champion Nello Pagani take the flag on another Condor at an average speed of 52 mph for the ultra-demanding course.

Another famous victory was chalked up in one of the final events run prior to Italy's entry into the Second World War in June 1940. This was the Milano-Taranto long-distance road race, when a Condor ridden by Guido Cerato was the first to take the chequered flag. Other renowned pre-war Condor riders included Alberto Ascari and Dorino Serafini.

## Dondolino

The year 1940 had also witnessed the début of a machine which, when racing resumed in Italy after the war in 1946, was to be the main antagonist of the big Guzzi singles in production racing events the – Gilera Saturno. However, when civilian production restarted it was evident that the men from Mandello had not been resting on their laurels. The Condor had received a new lease of life and a new name – Dondolino (rocking chair).

The most important change was more poke, now up to 106 mph on the street. Unkind critics suggested that the name 'Rocking Chair' stemmed from the result of the extra power on its handling, which was endowed with a rocking motion on fast corners. Despite this, the Guzzi was good enough for Enrico Lorenzetti to win the Swiss Grand Prix at Berne.

The following year saw several improvements, including a larger 260mm front stopper and a hand-crafted alloy mounting for the rear mudguard/racing number plate. There were also less important changes, including a front mudguard with shortened front section and

The first post-war hot Guzzi single, the Dondolino, which made its début in late 1945.

Dondolino engine assembly; note the exposed valve gear and hairpin springs.

stay at the bottom only, a larger 19-litre fuel tank and a choice of either a silencer or a straight racing pipe. The Dondolino was even lighter than the Condor, tipping the scales at 128kg in racing trim.

## Gambalunga
Guzzi built another machine alongside the sports racing Dondolino, the Gambalunga (long leg). Even more highly tuned and specialized, it was a pukka racing iron in every way, even if it came about by pure chance.

Factory tester Ferdinando Balzarotti had begun to demonstrate in the years immediately before the war that he was likely to develop into a first-class rider. When hostilities ended and racing resumed in Italy, Guzzi's famous racing designer Ing. Giulio Cesare Carcano was asked if he could do

something to help the young rider. In 1946, the 'something' emerged as the Gambalunga, for which Guzzi quoted a maximum speed of 112.5 mph.

The name came from the fact that, contrary to normal Guzzi practice, the engine's 90mm stroke was considerably greater than the bore of 84mm, making a 497.7cc long-stroke.

Still an overhead valve design, it was tuned to produce even more power than the Dondolino. In 1948 the bore and stroke reverted to the traditional big single 88×82mm and the usual capacity – the later type was referred to as the *Tipo Faenza*.

In performance there was little to choose between the two versions, although the Tipo Faenza developed its power at lower revs with consequently reduced engine stress.

The first engine type had a thick compression plate under the cylinder to

Enrico Lorenzetti en route to victory with his
Dondolino in the 1946 Swiss Grand Prix at Bern.

Bruno Francisci seen at the night start of the 1953 Milano-Taranto event. The same rider had earlier won the event on a Dondolino in both 1951 and 1952.

The even hotter Gambalunga appeared in 1947.

Crankcase and crankshaft from a Dondolino. Note the differing lengths of the con-rods for short and long-stroke engines.

compensate for the extra stroke (and a much longer connecting rod), but except for obvious compensatory changes such as re-working the crankcase mouth, there were no other structural differences between the two designs.

Early engines used the same cylinder head, but the later engine's casting had to be chamfered off to match up with the bore of the cylinder.

The valves were set at an angle of 60 degrees and were 46mm diameter for the outlet and 40mm for the sodium-filled exhaust valve. Both had 11mm split valve guides in bronze and exposed hairpin valve springs made of 4mm shot-peined wire.

Without doubt, this exposure contributed significantly to the wear suffered by the valve components, as on all such designs.

The most irritating feature of the Gambalunga was the need for constant adjustment of pushrod length and rocker clearance. The constantly changing quality of fuel available to the racing fraternity in the immediate post-war years made it necessary to change the compression ratio frequently by fitting compression plates, which upset the pushrod adjustment.

German rider Erhard Lienke warming up his
Dondolino in readiness for an 'Old Timer' racing
event at the Nürburgring in 1987.

This was compounded by the different coefficients of expansion of the barrel, valves and pushrods, which made it necessary to adjust for different engine temperatures as well.

The problem was so acute that when the correct racing clearances were set and the engine allowed to cool, both valves were lifted right off their seats. This meant that a peculiar cold starting drill was necessary: the tappet adjusting screws were slackened off, the engine was warmed, stopped and then the tappets were reset.

When one considers that the poor rider (for most Continental Circus performers went without the luxury of a mechanic) had to perform this task perhaps as many as six times a day, it is easy to imagine that it became a major source of annoyance.

Spectators were frequently treated to a first-hand lesson in the technique, as many a Guzzi competitor would carry out the ritual on the start line just before a race began.

Some riders discovered that by using pushrods from the three-wheel Guzzi Ercole light truck a cure was found to this problem. The Ercole employed 10×1mm steel pushrods. The ends were of a different design to the racer's components and the total weight of these pushrods was much lower.

The three-ring piston of the Gambalunga, with its almost flat top and lavish ribbing under the crown, offered a normal compression ratio of 8:1. Its 20mm gudgeon pin ran on a bronze bush pressed into the eye of the con-rod, which was made of chrome-nickel steel and had a split big-end eye running on uncaged steel rollers, a system used on the 500 Guzzi roadsters but considered impractical by many other manufacturers.

In practice it worked well enough for Moto Guzzi and had the additional advantage for a racing engine in the hands of a private rider that it was unnecessary to realign the crank flywheels on a rebuild – unlike the majority of contemporary high-performance racing singles which used one-piece con-rods and caged roller bearings in built-up flywheels.

On the low 73-octane fuel of the era the standard compression ratio on both types of engine produced 34 bhp at the rear wheel. The Tipo Faenza peaked at around 5500 rpm, against the original Gambalunga's 5800. Both were 'safe' to 6000. If this ceiling was exceeded by any considerable margin the result could be a cracked crankcase...

There was a further feature of the Gambalunga which marked it out from the Condor or Dondolino, for it was fitted with Guzzi's own design of leading-link front fork. Used on all Gambalungas made, this later became standard issue on the factory's GP bikes of the 1950s.

The Gambalunga's greatest track success came with Lorenzetti in the saddle. Following several victories on a Dondolino he rode a Gambalunga in 1948 and 1949, winning the 1949 Italian Grand Prix and both the Swiss and Ulster classics in 1948.

When one considers that Guzzi were campaigning a series of works V-twins at the time, these results, gained after all by a *production* racer, were nothing short of amazing.

## What to look for

All the Guzzi 'Gentleman racers' were limited-run machines built by the best engineering skills available to the factory at the time. And all, with the possible exception of the GTC, are today extremely valuable – almost on a direct par with classics such as the Manx Norton or AJS 7R. So one in original, fully serviceable condition is going to be expensive. Obviously it just might be possible to find one in need of restoration or as a basket case at a cheap figure.

Another problem will be parts, or lack of them. Much of the production racers' specification differed considerably from their roadster brothers, and not just brake hubs, close-ratio gears or forged pistons either. Many of the components were manufactured in special materials and will prove hyper-expensive if replacements are needed as they will have to be made as 'one-offs'.

But probably the biggest headache will be the original lighting equipment, kickstarter and other ancillaries, which were junked long ago when the majority of the bikes were raced in open events during their careers.

Anyone contemplating a Condor, Dondolino or Gambalunga, needs two things: a supportive bank manager and a lot of patience.

**Star Rating**
GTC four firm stars; Condor, Dondolino or Gambalunga five full stars

The value of these machines is already largely established and will continue to rise. Even so, if one can find (and afford) an example, I still rate it as a best buy. Few motorcycles offer such old world charm and true classic status.

# CHAPTER 4

# Airone

| | | |
|---|---|---|
| *** | **Airone Turismo** | **1939-57** |
| **** | **Airone Sport** | **1949-57** |

## History

The first Airone (Heron) appeared on the very eve of the Second World War in July 1939. Its 247cc (70×64mm) ohv engine and tubular frame revealed that it was a development of the earlier PE model. During 1939 and 1940 some 997 examples were manufactured, but following Italy's entry into the war in June 1940 production was halted to concentrate on military needs.

Production resumed in 1946 and the following year an updated version with many new features, notably telescopic front forks, improved brakes and a more modern style, was introduced. This was to prove the definitive type and remained available until 1957.

## Airone Turismo and Sport

The post-war Airone had several other

Moto Guzzi Airone photographed in Switzerland at
a rally for classic cars.

changes besides those outlined above. These included an aluminium cylinder head and barrel (the latter with a steel liner), enclosed rocker gear (from the 1948 model year), a modified frame, new exhaust system (still with 'fish-tail' silencer) and several more minor improvements.

Until 1949, only a single version was offered, except for military/police models. Then came the Sport. Compared to the standard bike, now named Turismo, the sportster provided its potential customers with a much improved level of performance and soon established itself as a firm favourite, with its 13 bhp at 6000 rpm against the Turismo's 9.5 bhp at 4800 rpm. The maximum speeds were 73 and 59 mph respectively.

Even so, cosmetically, and indeed technically in many aspects, the two models shared much in common. The horizontal pushrod unit construction engine featured dry-sump lubrication, with a 2-litre triangular container carried directly underneath the 10.5-litre fuel tank, and a gear-type pump mounted externally on the offside of the engine. The compression ratios, however, were different, 7:1 for the Sport, as against only 6:1 for the 'cooking' version. Both pistons were of similar design, with four rings (two oil scrapers, one below the 16mm gudgeon pin). The forged-steel connecting-rod featured a split, bolted-up section and uncaged rollers for the big-end, and a phosphor-bronze bush for the small-end. Other differences between the two power units included the thickness of hairpin valve springs (although the valves were identical at 33mm diameter for both models) and the carburettors (Turismo: Dell'Orto SBF 22; Sport: SS1 25A).

The gearing was also revised. Although the internal gearbox ratios of the two bikes were identical, first 2.6:1; second 1.788:1; third 1.34:1; and fourth 1:1, the Turismo used a 13-tooth gearbox sprocket and 43-tooth rear to give an overall ratio of 3.3:1. On the Sport the ratio was 3.07:1 as a result of specifying a 14-tooth gearbox sprocket. Primary drive was by helical gear with gearing of 36-65, providing a ratio of 1.805:1, and the wet clutch had a total of 10 plates.

The frames of the Turismo and Sport differed, with the Sport version in tubular steel while the Turismo was partly made up from pressings. A large roll-on centre-stand

A 250 Airone of the 1950s in military guise at the 1985 BMF Rally at Peterborough.

Four photographs from the Airone factory manual – almost as rare as the bikes themselves.

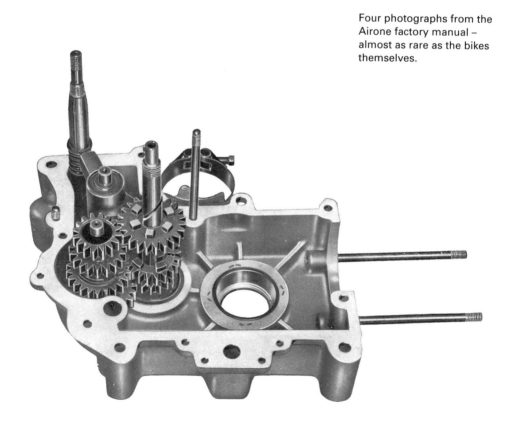

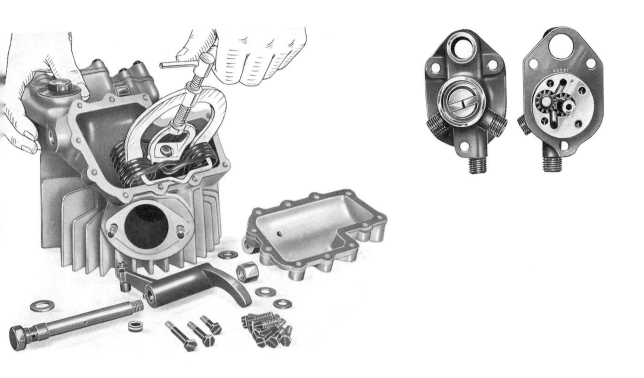

was fitted which, unlike the majority of those on modern Guzzi V-twins, was extremely sturdy *and* easy to operate. All variants of the post-war Airone featured deeply valanced mudguards front and rear, and several (even Sports) came with legshields as original equipment. A range of adjustment for the rider's position was provided by both the almost-flat handlebar and footrests, the latter having a pair of thick rubbers inscribed with the 'Moto Guzzi' logo.

## What to look for

Generally all versions of the Airone are blessed with a high standard of reliability. But not even the Sport can be described as a road burner – although what performance there is can be used to the full if one so desires.

Roadholding and braking of the Sport more than match its maximum speed. In addition the Turismo is a perfectly adequate machine, provided that you choose one with telescopic forks, the larger 180mm brakes and the enclosed valve gear.

The engine is also considerably smoother than the contemporary Guzzi 500 and considerably less stressed.

## Star rating: Airone Turismo three stars; Airone Sport four stars

Appearance of the post-war 1947 onwards Airone is very much akin to the 500 Falcone, so only someone familiar with Guzzi singles will know your bike is in fact only a 250. The Airone was also an almost bullet-proof design, so unless you are exceptionally unlucky you should not have many technical problems.

In many ways it is an undervalued bike, but conversely never likely to fetch the top money. Buy to ride, rather than as a 'bank vault' investment.

Another photograph from the Airone factory manual.

# CHAPTER 5

# Big Singles

| | | |
|---|---|---|
| *** | GTV & GTW | 1945-48 |
| *** | Astore | 1949-53 |
| **** | Falcone | 1950-67 |
| * | Falcone Nuovo | 1969-76 |

## History

Something which delivers its power stroke every other lamp-post is how most of us view the large-capacity lumbering four-stroke single of yesteryear. And it was a format which dominated motorcycling for the first half of the 20th century. Like Norton in England, Guzzi stuck to the traditional big single long after most other manufacturers had switched to twins, and during the immediate post-Second World War period the lakeside Mandello del Lario factory turned out a number of '500s', including the GTV, GTW, Astore and, the most famous of them all, the Falcone. The last named was destined, albeit in updated form, to outlast all the others of its genre. The Falcone Nuovo of 1976 represented the final production run of the old-fashioned big single anywhere in the world, and is not to be confused with modern offerings such as the Yamaha SR500 or Honda XBR 500 models.

## GTV, GTW

Both the GTV and GTW were basically the same machines that had appeared first as the 1934 Tipo V, and slowly improved over the years up to the outbreak of war. Like all Guzzi big roadster singles they were powered by an overhead valve 498.4cc engine. When peacetime production resumed in late 1945 both the GTV and GTW continued in the pre-war guise, but both were modernised in 1947 with telescopic front forks, larger brakes (only on the GTW), deeply valanced mudguards and modified rear suspension. In fact, both followed a similar development path to the 250 Airone (see Chapter 4), although there *were* differences, the most noticeable of which was that, unlike the smaller bike, both 500s retained cast-iron heads and barrels with exposed valve gear until the end of production. The GTV had its pre-war twin exhaust pipes and silencers deleted in favour of the simpler (and cheaper) set-up employed on the GTW.

There was a substantial difference in performance. The softer GTV with its 5.5:1 compression ratio produced 19 bhp at a lowly 4300 rpm, as opposed to the more sporting GTW, which gave 22 bhp at the slightly higher 4500 rpm and 6.5:1 compression ratio. Both models featured four-ring Borgo pistons despite the differing compression ratios, and both shared the same 12-plate clutches and 4-speed gearboxes. Maximum speeds were 70 mph and 81 mph respectively.

Externally, there was even less to distinguish the two. The fork bottoms were different and the GTW's wheels had the luxury of valanced alloy rims. Another pointer was the tyres, which on the GTV were both 3.50 × 19in, while the GTW employed a narrower section 3.25 at the

Changes from earlier models seen on the 1949 500 GTV included telescopic front forks and revised rear suspension.

A mid-1950s Falcone Sport on display at the 1979 Earls Court Show. Note the spares also in the photograph, which included a saddle, cylinder head and barrel, valves, piston, pushrods and other smaller components. The bike had been rebuilt by Guzzi enthusiast Terry Haynes.

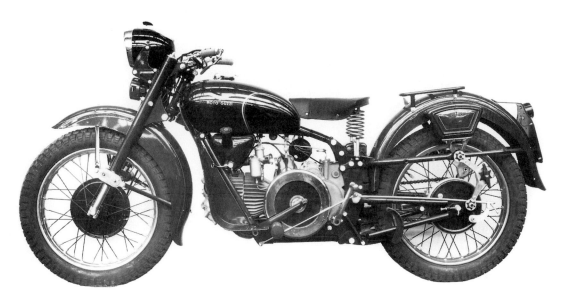

Falcone *Polizia* model circa 1959.

front. Both models were fitted out as standard with leg-shields, 'fish-tail' silencers, single-sprung saddles, a 6-volt 30-watt magneto/dynamo and 12-amp/hour batteries. A further variation was a single-seat, colour-matched sidecar (a pukka Guzzi accessory), either supplied separately or as a complete package fitted to the GTV model.

Both the big singles were again updated – and this time renamed as the Astore and Falcone respectively – at the end of the 1940s.

### Astore

The GTV was replaced for the 1949 season by the Astore (Goshawk). This incorporated several important modifications already tested and proved on the Airone: an alloy cylinder head and barrel, and enclosed rocker gear and brakes of larger diameter (as fitted to the GTW). However, the rest of the engine remained as for the GTV, as did the power output. The only other change was the fitment of the improved Dell'Orto MD2 carburettor.

The final variant produced in 1953 before the Astore was deleted at the end of the year saw a new Marelli MCR 4E magneto incorporating automatic advance/retard and

replacing the original MCR 4B with manual control.

### Falcone

The famous Italian motorcyling journalist Carlo Perelli called it 'The most romantic machine of them all'. He was of course referring to the Falcone (Hawk). By 'romantic' Perelli meant that it was a vintage-looking machine which retained features which had completely disappeared from designs of the previous decade and more (he was writing in the mid-1960s).

Chief amongst these features was the terrific pulling power provided by a big slow-revving engine – in other words an abundance of torque. Introduced in 1950 as the definitive version of Carlo Guzzi's 1920s-type horizontal single, the Falcone was offered in both Turismo (touring) and Sport form. But, except for the state of engine tune, the two were virtually identical.

By the late 1950s sales had slowed, and Guzzi discontinued selling the Falcone for civilian use, although they maintained production for the police and military authorities. But there were so many demands for its reintroduction that the company started listing it again at the end of

One Italian enthusiast's attempt to transform a 'cooking' Falcone into a fire-breathing Dondolino replica — it certainly worked from an appearance standpoint.

1963 at a price (in Italy) of 423,000 lire (around £240 at the exchange rates of the time).

In standard form none of the Falcones could be described as a sports bike (not even the so-called Sport). Its real forté was its ability to revive a pre-war atmosphere for its rider in the way it could potter along a quiet country lane at near walking pace in *top* gear, or, still in top, successfully tackle long mountain climbs and acute hairpin bends with the engine turning over so slowly that it was possible to count the individual power strokes.

Another outstanding feature was its ability to be ridden flat against the stop for mile after

The Falcone motor had the advantage over earlier Guzzi big singles of enclosed valve gear.

mile, without the least sign of fatigue and without the engine's beautiful oil-tightness being affected. So well within its limits did the Falcone function that truly vast mileages could be achieved without the need for a major engine overhaul. All these features were also why it proved so popular with the police and military authorities. Set against all these virtues, however, was its low maximum speed, which was around 80 mph in standard trim.

This prompted several red-blooded Italian enthusiasts to 'soup-up' their Falcones. In this they were helped by the fact that the customer racing models such as the Condor and Dondolino (see Chapter 3) were closely related to the roadster.

As set out in Chapter 3 the 'Gentleman Racer' lineage had begun in 1937 with the GTC, soon followed by the Condor. Then

Part of a factory brochure for the 1972 *Nuevo*
Falcone. It had been considerably updated, but was
nowhere near as reliable as the original.

after the war the faster Dondolino and later the quicker still Gambalunga. Meanwhile, as already recounted, the 'cooking' GTV was given an alloy head and barrel, became the Astore, and after the adoption of the Condor-type gear cluster and other bottom-end refinements the GTW became the Falcone.

Significantly, from the cylinder head/barrel down, the Falcone and Condor engines (and hence the Dondolino) were virtually identical in all but minor details and *material*. The crankcases, for instance, were absolutely indistinguishable except for the engine number and their *weight* – the Condor's were in elektron-magnesium alloy, while the Falcone's were plain aluminium-alloy. The cylinder head was similar with regard to port size and shape, valve sizes and other technical aspects, but the racers had exposed valve springs, whereas the Falcone (like the Astore) had all its oily bits decently covered.

What all this meant was that a Falcone could be made to go. From the standard machine's 80-odd miles per hour, it could be made to fly with a Dondolino cam, piston and carb, with the souped-up engine being capable of well in excess of the magic 'ton'. Here, in fact, lies one of the reasons why the Falcone was to gain such esteem – much as BSA's legendary Gold Star did in Britain.

From its introduction in 1950, the Falcone changed very little over the years, and in any case, except for its larger 29mm Dell'Orto carburettor, alloy head and barrel, together with the much 'cleaner' enclosed valve gear, it followed largely the same state of tune as the machine it replaced, the GTW.

In the appearance stakes, the Falcone definitely had an edge over its forerunner, with a new lower frame, more curvaceous 17.5-litre tank, a pillion pad in place of the original metal mudguard-top carrier, almost flat, narrow 'bars' and no leg shields.

Improved electrics were another bonus. The dynamo was now a 60-watt Marelli DN36, geared at 1.33:1 and with an IR39 regular from the same manufacturer; the battery had also been uprated to 13.5 amp/hour. On the original Falcone, the magneto featured manual advance and retard, but this was replaced in 1952 by an automatic unit.

For the 1954 model year the place of the now discontinued Astore was taken over by a lightly detuned version of the Falcone. It was then that both variants were given the Sport and Turismo tags. Emulating the Astore, this derivative had smaller valves, a 5.5:1 compression ratio and a 27mm Dell'Orto carburettor. However, both the gearbox and primary drive ratios remained the same; but the rear wheel sprocket had three more teeth, dropping the final drive ratio to 2.437:1.

Most Turismo models were sold with leg shields, and other differences included level of finish; the 'Sport' had more chrome work, such as the knee sections on the tank, whereas the Turismo had the cheaper paint instead.

Officially, the last 'civilian' Falcone was built in 1967, although for many years afterwards a steady stream of ex-police and military machines was offered to the public by dealers in Italy once they had reached the end of their service life.

Many imagined that this would be the end of the large-capacity big single from Guzzi, but they were wrong. Guzzi, like BMW more recently with their long-running flat-twins, were forced to reintroduce the concept due to public outcry. The result was the Falcone Nuovo (New).

**Falcone Nuovo**
Initial reports of the new Falcone, at first chiefly aimed at governmental sales, appeared in the Italian press during November 1969, with a prototype displayed later that month on the company's stand at the Milan Show.

This really was a new bike and just about the only thing it owed to the original was its 498.4cc capacity with its traditional Guzzi 88×82mm bore and stroke dimensions. This was no mere recycling of the old bike, but a completely new expression of the classic horizontal flat-single, both from an engine and running gear point of view.

As far as the mechanical components were concerned there was now an integral finned 3-litre wet sump – so the oil tank was no

The final variant of the Falcone line, the Sahara,
offered between 1974 and 1976.

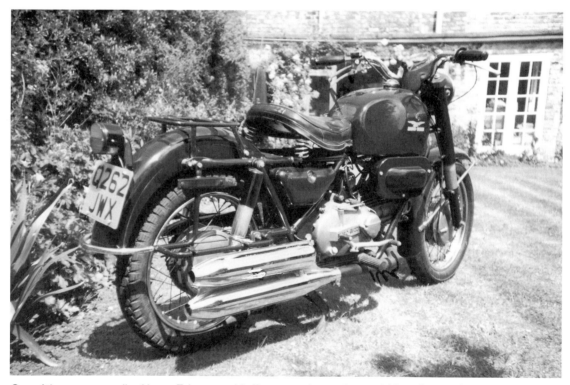

One of the many ex-police Nuevo Falcones sold off
to private buyers. Potential owners should be aware
that these bikes can be a potential landmine. Not
only was the model less than perfect mechanically,
but some ex-police machines have been sold
showing less mileage than actually covered.

more, a square slide VHB 29A carburettor replaced the earlier (now obsolete) round slide instrument, the engine, gearbox and clutch were now unified in a more modern way, giving the power unit a totally new and updated appearance. And much work had been expanded on the various internals. But all this was to little avail in providing the 'Nuovo' model with any more poke than the original, as the power output of the 1970s Falcone was only 26.2 bhp at 4800 rpm.

Customers would probably have accepted this had the *reliability* matched the original model. Sadly, it did not. Many informed enthusiasts considered the redesigned model a mere shadow of a once great motorcycle and several even voiced the opinion that it suffered 'from lack of development'. Faults included oil not getting up in sufficient quantity to the inlet tappet, thereby allowing the rocker to wear away the end of the valve stem; it is common to remove the tappet inspection cover and find the valve spring retainer dry and covered with the fine red dust of powdered steel.

Another problem is burnt exhaust valves and buckled valve seats. On some machines valve seats have been known to fall out of the heads. Yet another fault is the oil screen in the sump, which is made of pressure die-cast 'pot' metal that often crumbles into tiny pieces and metal shrapnel in the oil circulation system does not contribute to the longevity of the component parts! All-in-all the Falcone Nuovo engine is something of a time bomb, waiting to catch the unwary... you have been warned.

All this is a great pity, as the cycle parts are so much better than those of the original. For example the frame was a brand new double-cradle tubular-steel structure, with fully enclosed front and rear suspension, and full-width 220mm diameter Grimeca drum brakes (a twin-leader at the front). At 185kg (407 lb) dry, the new Falcone was some 15kg heavier than the original, but in its favour were its improved handling and braking, powerful 12-volt electrics and press-button starting.

The government contract bikes were either supplied in khaki green or dark blue, the civilian models in red and white. From 1974 onwards a new 'civvy' model, the Sahara, was offered. This was finished in a new sand and black finish, and came with crashbars, panniers and engine side covers.

The concept of the Falcone Nuovo was good, but it was a terrible pity about that awful engine! Probably because of a mounting list of warranty claims Guzzi axed production at the end of 1976. From then on it concentrated its efforts on its badge engineered Benelli-based models and the popular and reliable V-twins.

## What to look for

Generally the Guzzi big singles are the epitome of reliability, *except* for the problems outlined above which are peculiar to the Nuovo Falcone. So I would advise anyone to think very carefully before purchasing one of the latter machines. In addition to this you need to be careful about machines imported from Italy. Make sure you can trace the bike's history, otherwise you may be buying a 'tarted-up' ex-military or police bike. This is not to say that all ex-government bikes should be avoided, just that variances between different examples are so much greater than with comparable civilian models.

**Star rating – Falcone: four stars; GTV, GTW and Astore: three stars; Falcone Nuovo rates only a single star because of its poor reliability record**
The original Falcone is a true classic amongst Italian bikes and only its long production run stops it getting five stars. The cooking models are still good bikes, but without the glamour, hence their 'middle-of-the-road' three stars. As for the poor old Nuovo, it is best left alone – its solitary star reflects this.

# Galletto

| ** | Galletto 160 | 1950-52 |
|----|--------------|---------|
| *** | Galletto 175 | 1952-53 |
| *** | Galletto 192 | 1954-60 |
| ** | Galletto 192 Elettrico | 1961-66 |

**History**

If Britain can boast of its Bantam, then Guzzi buffs can point to the Galletto ('cockerel'). Like the BSA product, it was inspired by the motorcycle sales boom which swept through the immediate post-war days and lasted until the mid-1950s.

In pre-war days the Italian manufacturers (as did the British) catered largely for the enthusiast market and therefore the demand was for road burners, rather than commuter bikes. However, the end of hostilities brought with it a shortage of new cars, high prices of second-hand vehicles and rapidly rising running costs – factors which caused 'utility' users to take to two wheels when their normal preference would have been for the cheap, mass-produced car.

Many motorcycle manufacturers both in Italy and abroad responded to this new-found market by producing a swarm of lightweight two-stroke motorcycles of 125cc and below, and others (largely non-bike builders) such as Innocenti and Piaggio churned out thousands of scooters.

But there was a third concept, which saw the combination of motorcycle and scooter practice aimed at 'providing the best of both worlds'. Examples were the German Maico Mobil and the British Velocette LE. However, one country really excelled in this particular sphere, and this was Italy.

A whole host of motorcycle-scooter hybrids made an appearance between 1949 and 1954. They included the MV Pullman (Mk I), Motom Delfino, Macchi Zeffiro, Rumi Scoiattolo and the Guzzi Galletto.

**Galletto**

It is largely agreed that the Mandello offering was the best of the bunch. This is confirmed in the following extract from the British weekly *Motorcycling*, dated 24 June, 1952: 'the adoption of new techniques has meant mainly the incorporation of lessons learned from motor-scooters. The outstanding example of this is the Guzzi Galletto, which, while unquestionably a motorcycle, has 'borrowed' scooter ideas to a great extent. It retains the obvious advantages of the motorcycle – large wheels giving stability and freedom from roll and, thanks to the horizontal engine, a weight distribution giving good front-wheel adhesion. To that has been married the scooter's attributes of near-perfect weather protection and mechanical enclosure. The riding position, behind the large front shield, allows good control, while space for parcel carrying is provided on top of the engine shielding. Once again footboards have been chosen instead of footrests, while an innovation at the time of the model's introduction was the carrying of a spare wheel – surely the first time that such an item had figured in the

# GIUDIZI
# DELLA STAMPA INTERNAZIONALE

## "Galletto"
150 cc.

**Soc. p. Az. MOTO GUZZI - Mandello del Lario (Como)**

*Lubrificanti SHELL*                         **Gomme PIRELLI**

Factory leaflet for the 1950 pre-production 150cc Galletto. This scooter-cum-motorcycle enjoyed a 16-year production life span and proved exceptionally reliable in service.

Following capacity increases to first 160, then
175cc, the Galletto was finally enlarged to 192cc in
early 1954.

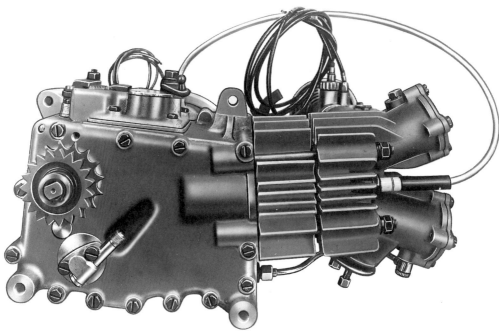

The Galletto engine unit. Early versions had three
speeds, but the 175 and 192cc models featured an
extra cog.

standard equipment of any solo motorcycle as distinct from a scooter'.

The prototype Galletto was revealed to the public at the Geneva Show in March 1950 and created a lot of interest. By the time production had started later that year the 150cc engine of the prototype had been increased to 159.5cc (62×53mm). Production was soon up to some 3000 units per month, and it made a major contribution to the factory's output during the early 1950s.

The Galletto's specification included a purpose-built ohv four-stroke engine, car-type exhaust system, 3-speed gearbox, dry-sump lubrication, chain final drive, a frame with a tubular steel main spar with sheet metal pressings around the engine and leading link front forks. The rear suspension had the unusual feature of a single rear fork. Both wheels were fully interchangeable and carried 17 in tyres.

At the end of 1952, the engine was increased in capacity to 174.4cc (65×53mm) and power output upped from 5.6 bhp to 7 bhp. But without doubt the most relevant improvement was the addition of a fourth gear ratio − in answer to the many moans from customers who said the original 3-speed box with its widely spaced ratios did not provide the means of maintaining a useful pace out on the open road.

Further changes came early in 1954, including another increase in engine capacity to 192cc (65×58mm), achieved this time by an increase in stroke, rather than bore size. Other modifications were a higher compression ratio and a larger carburettor (Dell'Orto MA19 BSI). Although the power output was raised by a puny 0.5 bhp, the larger unit did provide a useful increase in engine torque.

The introduction of the '192' brought some useful improvements to other aspects of the machine. Although the electrics remained 6-volt, they were uprated with a Marelli DN36 A45/62200 D dynamo and three-pole IR26 A-45/6 voltage regulator which sat atop the crankcase assembly. At the same time the battery was exchanged for a more powerful 12-amp component, and a larger 150mm headlamp with a higher wattage 35/40 bulb fitted. Fuel capacity went up to 8.5 litres with

1 litre in reserve, and a grab handle for the pillion was fixed between the two seats. In all its basic essentials, however, the Galletto remained unaltered.

The last redesign came in time for the 1961 season. Although the engine size stayed as before, power was increased slightly by upping the compression to 7:1. In addition the final drive gear ratio was changed to 3.26:1 by the fitment of a smaller, 15-tooth gearbox sprocket. Major changes, however, were applied to the machine's bodywork, rear suspension and electrical system. Cosmetically, the Galletto was restyled in a clear attempt to cash in on the likes of the best-selling Lambretta Li series 2 and TV scooters, with a fully enclosed cast-alloy shell for the headlamp (which incidentally was *reduced* in size to 130mm) and the central section of the handlebars, which now hid the control cables from view. This might have been fine cosmetically, but made maintenance far less easy than before!

Not only were the headlamp and handlebar controls altered, but the steering column and front mudguard were given a much more streamlined appearance, with the guard carrying deep valances. Again, to provide a more marketable appearance, a two-tone dualseat and considerably larger rear lights were specified. The latter, like the headlamp, was very much as one would have found on a Lambretta (or Vespa) of the period.

Underneath the revised panelling, the rear suspension was considerably updated with a massive, single, upright and hydraulically damped suspension leg at the rear of the swinging-arm fork, which otherwise remained almost unchanged from the original employed on the 1950 prototype.

Another item to receive attention was the exhaust system, but perhaps the most important improvement was to the electrics. For the first time a 12-volt system and electric start were employed on a Guzzi two-wheeler. A crankshaft-mounted generator was linked by a pulley and belt to a Marelli 75-watt DNT 2A/75/12/3 dynastart unit on the rear nearside of the engine; a special metal cover was fitted to cover the drive belt. The voltage regulator used with this system

A Galletto in Guzzi's wind tunnel during the
mid-1950s. The spare wheel mounting could hardly
have been *less* aerodynamic!

The final variant, with revised appearance and specification was built between 1961 and 1966. Major differences included handlebar-mounted headlamp, dualseat and electric start. The capacity stayed at 192cc.

was a Marelli IER 2A unit, while to cope with the extra demand a heavy-duty 20-amp hour battery was fitted. Access to this was by lifting the hinged dualseat, which also covered the oil-tank filler cap. At 134kg (278lb), the 1961 electric start Galletto was much heavier than earlier versions.

This together with the 'copy-cat' styling borrowed from other manufacturers effectively changed the character of the machine, and although it might have been superior in some respects, it lost out to a larger degree in other areas.

What all Gallettos did possess was a long life, not only from a 16-year production run, but an excellent service record, unmatched by any other Italian two-wheeler of its era. Many of Guzzi's little 'cockerels' were still giving everyday service 20 or 30 years after they had left the production line, winning many admirers along the way. The Galletto is therefore a lasting testament that even a humble commuter bike can become a classic in its own right.

## What to look for
Because of the numbers manufactured and its high level of reliability, it is still possible to find plenty of Gallettos in their native land. However, outside the confines of Italy it's a different story. This means that most potential 'new owners' will have to import an example. Make sure you know what you are buying. Although it is a *real* classic of its type, it's still very much a commuter bike, not a sportster. Also it is important to make sure all the 'tin-ware' for the bodywork is intact, as this will be difficult, if not impossible, to locate elsewhere.

## Star rating: Two or three firm stars
Most of all the Galletto was an honest-to-goodness workhorse. This together with its long production life will limit its 'collectable value'. But if you are into *small* Italian bikes, it's well worth consideration.

## Conclusion
One for the masses, but a good one. Maximum speed was in the mid-fifties for all versions and increases in engine sizes only seemed to assist torque ratings.

# CHAPTER 7

# Lodola

| | | |
|---|---|---|
| *** | 175 Lodola | **1956-58** |
| *** | 175 Lodola Sport | **1958-59** |
| *** | 235 Lodola | **1959-66** |
| **** | Lodola Regolarita | **1959-63** |

**History**

The Lodola ('lark') was Carlo Guzzi's last design and it had many features to commend it, including a gentlemanly, unobtrusive personality; excellent handling and roadholding; a miserly fuel consumption; and, most interesting of all – it was manufactured in both ohc and ohv forms – in a variety of engine capacities.

As recounted in earlier chapters Moto Guzzi was the leading Italian motorcycle manufacturer in the decade from the end of the Second World War, until the mid-1950s. However, the following ten years were a period of rapid decline and it is unfortunate that the Lodola, launched at the Milan Fair in April 1956, was largely unable to provide a solution to Guzzi's ever increasing problems.

In the years preceding the Lodola's public début, Moto Guzzi did not have a machine to compete in the all-important 175cc roadster category. Rival makes such as Bianchi, MV Agusta, Parilla and Gilera all had suitable bikes – Guzzi nothing.

**175**

Carlo Guzzi and his team of engineers realized from an early stage that if the new machine was to make any headway against its established rivals it had to come up with something special. So they opted for a chain-driven overhead camshaft, but with a cylinder inclined 45 degrees from the vertical, full unit construction and a modern chassis and suspension. The initial Lodola's exact engine size was 174.4cc (62×57.8mm). Guzzi opted to drive the overhead cam by a chain running up the offside of the engine, totally enclosing it within the alloy cylinder casting. It was equipped with a small damping stabiliser which was tensioned at all engine speeds and temperatures by an automatic adjuster.

The cylinder head was also an alloy casting, above which was a single large finned 'dome' which could be removed to provide access to the valve gear. The valves were closed by paired coil springs and split collet retainers, and were operated by rocker arms with simple screw and locknut tappet adjusters. These rockers were housed in a detachable one-piece cast-iron holder which pivoted from the cylinder head and was mounted on springs so as to provide automatic compensation for variations in tappet clearance.

The engine employed a dry-sump lubrication system with a separate oil tank on the nearside of the frame matching a hinged battery box (containing a 6-volt 10 amp hour unit) on the offside. Inside the oil tank was a detachable, washable strainer, and there was an additional, similar filter on the offside of the crankcase which could be reached by removing the outer engine casing. Oil was circulated by a gear-driven pump, and an

The Lodola was Carlo Guzzi's final design. The 175 shown here featured an ohc engine.

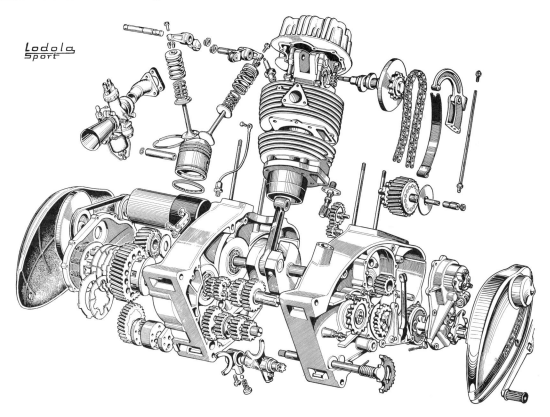

*Lodola Sport*

Details of the 175 Lodola engine. Note the chain drive to the overhead camshaft, geared primary drive and belt-driven dynamo.

external oil pipe ran up the rear of the cylinder barrel to provide top-end lubrication.

The oil pump was housed behind the inner engine casing on the nearside of the crankcase, together with the primary drive gear and the wet multi-plate clutch. The front primary drive gear was an unusual design, for it was manufactured in two parts, an inner and an outer, between which were fitted a series of small rubber bushes the purpose of which was to act as a transmission shock absorber; the two sections were held together by a large circlip.

The outer casing on the left of the engine was dry, and housed a massive steel flywheel and dynamo drive, consisting of a pulley wheel on the crankshaft driving a second wheel on the dynamo itself via a belt. The dynamo was mounted at the front of the crankcase and was fully enclosed by the engine cover.

The performance of the machine was very much that of other Italian bikes of the same class. During its 10 July, 1959, road test *Motor Cycling* achieved a maximum speed of 61 mph (Guzzi claimed 68 mph) and an overall fuel consumption of 82 mpg, including the speed testing section.

A sport version followed in 1958 and this was essentially the same bike, but in a higher state of tune and with a couple of changes to the styling and general specification. The compression ratio was upped to 9:1 and fitting a hotter cam increased power output from 9 to 11 bhp, taking the top speed to almost 75 mph. There was a larger, more bulbous tank holding 16 litres (12 litres on the standard version) and fitted with a quick-release chrome cap. Finally the Sport received alloy instead of chrome wheel rims.

From 1959 onwards the 175 Sport was equipped with more powerful polished-alloy full-width brake hubs, and a more sporting style was also achieved by an attractive Italian racing red paint job.

### 235

The year 1959 also saw the standard touring model receive a capacity increase, to 235cc. But this was no simple larger bore job, as both the bore *and* stroke were changed – to

Guzzi achieved considerable success in the ISDT with the Lodola. All the pukka trials mounts sported ohc and were produced in 175, 235 *and* 250cc engine sizes. The last was never offered as a road bike.

From 1959 the standard production road-going Lodola was offered as a 235cc with pushrod-operated valves. It remained in production until 1966. Only the Gran Turismo version was built (except, of course, the specialized trials bike).

68 and 64mm respectively. Another major alteration was the substitution of the overhead-cam valve gear by pushrod operation. There were other constructional differences too: the cylinder barrel was now of cast iron while the carburettor finally received an efficient air filtration system.

Named the Gran Turismo, the 235 had the same 7.5:1 compression ratio as the standard 175 which it superseded. With 11 bhp on tap, the newcomer was slower (at 72 mph) than the 175 Sport, but provided its rider with a definite improvement in engine flexibility. The appearance, except for chrome wheel rims and a slightly different coach-lining pattern, the 235 Lodola Gran Turismo was identical to the 175 Sport.

It is worth including the following extract from *The Motor Cycle* of 3 March, 1960, to illustrate the nature of the machine: 'The predominating impression on the Moto Guzzi is of a gentlemanly, unobtrusive performance. Yet when the whip was used, the engine would respond with a willingness amply matched to the exuberance of the rider's mood. As if to contradict the rakish appearance of the downward-swept handlebar and the recessed, 3½-gallon fuel tank, the model proved extremely quiet. Exhaust and induction muffling were of a high order and mechanical noise was virtually nil. Everything seemed *muted*. The helical-gear primary drive emitted a slight whine, never unduly pronounced, when the

A 1963 235 Gran Turismo; note the deeply valanced mudguarding, full-width alloy hubs, peaked headlamp rim and square Italian tax holder.

oil was warm. Noise from the valve gear amounted to no more than a faint rustle.'

## Regolarita

After Guzzi quit road racing at the end of 1957, it switched its sporting attentions to trials. Over the next few years it built a number of machines based around the Lodola in Regolarita (Enduro) trim in 175, 235 and 247cc engine sizes – the last capacity was never used on the standard production models and all three engine sizes used ohc.

There were a number of other differences between the roadsters and these off-road dirt irons. First of all, although they shared the same basic frame layout, the Regolaritas had upright rear shocks instead of the inclined mounting on the roadsters. These were matched to much sturdier hydraulically damped front forks (all the Lodola roadsters employed undamped forks of a much flimsier design). The brake drums were the single-sided units from the original 175

Lodola touring model, with different rims and knobbly tyres, and in an attempt to reduce weight, items such as the oil and fuel tanks, and mudguards, were constructed in aluminium.

## What to look for

The vast majority of Lodolas manufactured were the 235 Gran Turismo, which enjoyed an eight-year production life from 1959 till the end of 1966. Both the 175 Standard and Sport, together with the works Regolarita trials models, are comparatively rare today, but only the dirt bike is really collectable.

## Star rating: three stars for the street, four for the dirt

A soundly engineered design rather than an exciting sportster limits the Lodola 'classic' appeal. The works dirt bikes earn an extra star rating due to their rarity and fitness for purpose – they scored a series of gold medal performances in the ISDT.

# CHAPTER 8

# Stornello

| | | |
|---|---|---|
| ** | Stornello 125 Turismo | 1960-68 |
| ** | Stornello 125 Sport | 1961-68 |
| *** | Stornello 125 ISDT | 1966 |
| ** | Stornello America | |
| | & Scramber 125 | 1967-75 |
| ** | Stornello 160 | 1968-75 |

## History

The Stornello was largely intended as a relatively cheap-to-produce lightweight with a pushrod single-cylinder engine, suitable as a commuter, ride-to-work machine requiring the minimum of maintenance and available at a low purchase price. It was also the first series production model from Guzzi's talented racing designer, Ing. Carcano, and made its début (125 Turismo) at the Milan Show in December 1959.

## 125

The 125 Stornello had a unit-construction engine with an exact capacity of 123.175cc (52×58mm). These long-stroke dimensions provided 7 bhp at 7000 rpm. Hardly earth shattering, but a hidden bonus was the design's wide spread of power and its forgiving nature.

The cylinder head and barrel were both of light alloy, the latter with a cast-iron liner, and inclined at 25 degrees. Inside the head, the combustion chamber was flat, with parallel valves. Following Lodola tradition, a single large rocker box was fitted to the top of the cylinder head and secured by a total of six Allen bolts. A single cast-iron rocker support held the rocker arms in position, with the valves themselves having single coil springs and easy-to-adjust tappets and locknuts.

The carburettor, a Dell'Orto ME18BS, was mounted on a long alloy inlet stub, which was secured to the cylinder head with a noticeable offset to the nearside. The exhaust pipe was offset by a similar amount at the front, so that the pipe ran outside the frame tubes on the offside of the bike. Access to the 14mm spark plug was gained through the downtubes, as the plug itself was located centrally right at the front of the head.

A flat-top Borgo piston provided a compression ratio of 8:1, and was equipped with four rings, including a second oil scraper below the gudgeon pin. This ran in a bronze small-end bush, with a diameter of 16mm, in the one-piece steel con-rod. The crankpin was a press-fit in the full-circle steel flywheels, and the big-end bearing consisted of 14 steel rollers in an alloy cage.

Like the vast majority of small Italian machines of the era the crankcase was split vertically and lubrication was pressure-fed through a gear pump. A change from usual Guzzi practice at the time was that wet-sump oil storage was used with a capacity of 1.5 litres (2.6 pints). There was a detachable oil filter strainer which was reusable simply by washing it in petrol prior to reassembly. In common with other Guzzi singles the primary drive was by helical gears to the multi-plate clutch, and the gearbox had four ratios.

Ignition was taken care of by a CEV flywheel magneto, which contained the points and condenser. An external HT coil

Intended as a cheap-to-produce, cheap-to-sell machine, the Stornello (shown here in 1962 Sport form) was originally powered by a 123.1cc ohv, 4-speed unit-construction engine.

was mounted under 12.5-litre fuel tank. The flywheel magneto also carried coils for the lighting circuit, rated at 6 volts, 28 watts. Although this charged a 7-amp/hour battery, lighting was direct, as the battery provided power to the horn only. The ignition and lighting switches were mounted in the 130mm Aprilia headlamp, together with a terminal board and diode.

The engine assembly formed a stressed member in the frame. Both wheel hubs were laced to 17 in rims. The brake hubs were of polished light-alloy wth a diameter of 135mm.

Initially only the Turismo was available, either with a dual-seat or single-sprung saddle. In late 1961 Guzzi introduced a lightly tuned version, the 125 Sport. This featured an engine with a hemispherical head, inclined valves and a higher compression (9.8:1) four-ring piston. Equipped with a larger UB20B carburettor, power output climbed to a heady 8.5 bhp. Cosmetically, the Sport's appearance was changed by fitting lower bars, a racing-style seat, abbreviated mudguards and alloy wheel rims. Although the tank's shape

remained similar, its capacity had been upped to 14.5 litres.

A specialized ISDT replica trials model was marketed briefly in very small numbers for the 1966 model year only. This was virtually a production version of the medal-winning works bikes of the early 1960s.

The following year, 1967, saw the 125 Scrambler and 125 Sport America introduced in place of the Sport and Turismo.

The 1967 machines *looked* considerably different, but in most cases the components used were from earlier models, blended in to the new. One of the few totally newly designed items was the dual-seat. Almost everything else, except the specialized parts fitted only to the Scrambler, was either from the original Sport or Turismo models. For instance, although the tank now had different graphics, it was the same 12.5-litre unit as on the 1960 Turismo. Likewise side panels and mudguards were from the Sport. To justify the 'America' section of the title, the 'new' Sport featured 'hi-and-wide' bars. Of course, there were minor changes: the rear shocks now wore trendy exposed chrome

# 125

**MOTO GUZZI**

*SPORT*

## SPECIFICATION

**ENGINE:** single cylinder, four stroke.

**CYLINDER:** made of light alloy with special cast iron inserted liner, inclined 25°.

**CYLINDER HEAD:** made of light alloy with valve gear in oil bath.

**VALVE OPERATION:** push rods and rockers.

**BORE:** 52 mm.

**STROKE:** 58 mm.

**DISPLACEMENT:** 125 cc.

**OUTPUT:** 12 HP

**COMPRESSION RATIO:** 9.8 to 1

**LUBRICATION:** oil sump in crankcase (about 1.9 litres - 0.502 gall. USA, 0.417 imp. gall.).

**OIL FILTERS:** Screen type in crankcase - centrifugal on crankshaft.

**FUEL TANK CAPACITY:** 15.5 litres (4.095 gall. USA - 3.409 imp. gall.) including 3 litres reserve (0.792 gall. USA - 0.66 imp. gall.)

**FUEL CONSUMPTION:** Litres 2.7 for 100 kms. (89 m.p.g. USA - 104 m.p.g. imp.) (measured according to CUNA standards).

**GEARBOX:** 4 speeds, foot operated.

**IGNITION:** flywheel alternator with external H.T. coil.

**SUSPENSION:** telescopic front fork with hydraulic dampers, rear swinging fork with coil springs in the hydraulic dampers.

**BRAKES:** expanding: front, hand operated; rear, foot operated.

**WHEELS:** 17x2 1/4'' rims.

**TYRES:** front 2½x17'' ribbed; rear 2.75-17R'' block tread.

**WEIGHT:** about 92 kgs. (203 lbs.)

**MAXIMUM SPEED:** over 70 m.p.h.

During the late 1960s and early 1970s the 125 Sport (sold Stateside as the Sport America) looked like this. Basic mechanics were unchanged from the original.

In late 1968 the Stornello appeared with a larger engine (153.24cc). Called the '160', this was in many ways Guzzi's answer to the contemporary Ducati

Monza Junior. Producing 13.6 bhp, maximum speed was 73 mph.

springs and the design of the forks had been slightly altered.

The Scrambler's looks differed only in having a high-level, silver-painted exhaust system based on the design employed on the ISDT bikes, a front mudguard with more clearance, braced bars, a stoneguard for the headlamp glass, a sump shield and more suitable tyres, a studded 2.75×17 in front and knobbly 3.00×17 in rear. The Scrambler also differed in its gearing, with a 15-tooth gearbox sprocket against the Sport's 16/47 ratio. With this lower ratio, maximum speed was 58 mph, compared to 70 mph for the roadster.

## 160

In late 1968 the Stornello was given a larger engine capacity (153.24cc). Called the '160', this was achieved by boring the cylinder out to 58mm. Very few other changes were made apart from a new 9:1 3-ring piston. Even the 20mm carburettor remained the same. To compensate for the extra performance (13.6 bhp) gearing was raised by fitting a 17-tooth gearbox sprocket. The 125s remained in production.

Externally, however, it is easy to tell the two

engines apart thanks to a bulge on the offside outer casing. This hid a major improvement, a 6-volt 60-watt CEV alternator, which replaced the typically feeble flywheel magneto electrics of the smaller version. To cope with this a 17-amp/hour battery was fitted, although the front and rear lights remained as before. There were also other changes. To match the higher engine output, a more powerful 157mm-diameter front brake was specified. Cosmetically, the tank, mudguards and side panels were also restyled, giving angular rather than rounded lines.

The 160 continued (together with the 125s) until 1971, when a new 5-speed gearbox was introduced for both engine capacities, and both underwent a major redesign – their first and only major change during their production life. As part of this, both Stornellos were henceforth to share common styling.

As well as the addition of an extra ratio, both engines reverted to inclined valves. More obvious externally was the recasting of the outer cases. Banished were the previous 'egg-like' smooth lines and in their place something much less attractive, ugly even.

Completing the line-up of Stornellos in 1968 was the 125 Scrambler: a cobby little mount based on the roadster, but with the looks of the factory ISDT bikes.

The final 160 Stornello looked like this. Besides new styling and modified engine covers, it now sported a 5-speed 'box'. It was offered between 1971 and 1974.

The nearside casing carried a gearbox for the newly specified tachometer, which took its drive from the end of the camshaft.

Strangely, the electrics reverted (probably for reasons of cost) to the 28-watt flywheel magneto, although the more powerful 17-amp/hour battery from the 160 was retained. Another change was the use of the then new square slide (22mm) VHB carburettor.

Much of the running gear had received attention. Although the frame was based on the original, it now featured a new upper mounting position for the rear shocks, giving them a more upright angle. The front forks were totally new, with the old-style spring covers gone in favour of the current trend towards exposed stanchions and internal springs (the Scrambler version was provided with rubber gaiters). There were new mudguards in polished stainless steel to replace the previous painted steel components.

The 160 was only offered in roadster form, and although this was identical in all but engine capacity to the smaller roadster both shared differences compared with the 125 Scrambler. As well as different forks, exhaust, handlebars, headlamp, seat, tank and mudguards, there were added a sump guard and knobbly tyres to complete the Scrambler's differing role and style.

The final year of full production for the Stornello range was 1974. There were a few, mainly cost-cutting, changes, including deletion of the tachometer and a different (slashed-end cone Lafraconi) silencer. In addition the rocker cover was recast, gaining for the first time conventional cooling fins and so giving the top of the engine a totally new appearance.

The last Stornello rolled off the production line in early 1975 after 15 years of continuous manufacture.

## What to look for
None of the Stornello models (except the ISDT Replica) is anything more than a basic commuter-type lightweight. But as such it is a robust little bike which is not prone to any particular weakness. There are still quite large numbers in Italy, but spares are likely to prove a problem, particularly for an owner wishing to *ride* rather than *show* his mount.

## Star ratings: ISDT Replica three stars, the remaining models two stars
Nothing to get too excited over here, for none of the series production Stornello models is ever going to be worth a large sum of money, not even the so-called 'Sport' version. Instead they are best regarded as an Italian version of the Triumph Terrier/Cub series.

The ISDT Replica is a thoroughbred specialized mount, which was capable of a class-leading performance in long-distance trials of the era, and therefore is a more collectable proposition to the few enthusiasts for this section of the sport.

# CHAPTER 9

# Early Vees

| | | |
|---|---|---|
| *** | V7 | 1967-76 |
| | (models after 1970 will be ex-military or police bikes and are worth one less star) | |
| **** | V7 Special/Ambassador | 1969-71 |
| **** | GT850/Eldorado | 1972-74 |
| ** | California | 1972-74 |
| ***** | V7 Sport | 1972-73 |
| **** | 750 Sport | 1974-75 |
| *** | 750 S3 | 1975-76 |

## History

The origins of the large-capacity V-twin Guzzi motorcycles came from the Mandello del Lario company's involvement with Italy's military and civil authorities. The V-twin engine itself started life not in a two-wheeler, but as the power unit of the amazing 3×3 lightweight military tractor. This was produced for the Italian army between 1960 and 1963 as a 'go-anywhere' machine and featured a 90-degree V-twin ohv engine of 754cc with a bore and stroke of 80×75mm. The power produced was only 20 bhp at 4000 rpm, but its massive torque made it ideal for its intended role. Other features included a single-plate dry clutch, a 6-speed gearbox and shaft final drive.

From this unlikely source was to come one of the truly classic Italian motorcycles of the post-war era. It was also the machine which was to put the company back on the road to success following a financial crisis in the mid-1960s.

## V7

Work on the first prototype of what was ultimately to emerge as the V7 (V=V-twin, 7=700cc) was started in 1964. Early the following year, the first pre-production models went up for governmental approval and soon after came official acceptance and the placing of contracts by both the police and military authorities. The success of these

tests prompted Guzzi to consider a civilian version, and this made its public appearance in December 1965 at the 39th Milan Show.

The work of the legendary Guzzi racing designer Ing. Giulio Carcano, the V7 was an imposing machine by any standards. And at the time of its appearance was also the biggest and fastest road-going machine ever to have come from the Guzzi factory.

As befits an engine originally designed for use by the military in the field, the V7's engine was created with the emphasis on simplicity and ease of maintenance. Many have since referred to it as 'agricultural', but none can question its undoubted strength. With an exact capacity of 703.717cc, this overhead valve power unit had over-square dimensions with a bore and stroke of 80×70mm. Running on a compression ratio of 9:1, it produced 50 bhp at a fairly leisurely 6000 rpm.

The engine layout provided excellent accessibility and this, combined with a relatively 'soft' state of tune, made for a long, maintenance-free life. These characteristics were to prove the design's strongest and most appealing features over the years. There were, however, one or two aspects which appeared to be at odds with the designer's priorities of a 'back-to-basics' engineering approach. One of these was the use of chrome-plated cylinder bores. These might be technically superior, offering closer

A very early production V7. This 1966 bike was directly derived from the first police and military versions. The V7 prefix was drawn from the engine's transverse 90-degree V-twin layout. The capacity was 703.717cc.

running tolerances and longer life (under ideal conditions), but have the disadvantage that if the bore become either worn or damaged, only a complete replacement barrel *and* piston will suffice – whereas a conventional cast-iron liner can be rebored several times, or have a new liner pressed in when the largest oversize has been used. Pistons and barrels were matched (and colour coded) at the factory in A, B and C sizes.

A one-piece steel crankshaft employed steel con-rods with bolt-up eyes running on split-shell white metal big-end bearings. Like the main bearings these were manufactured from AL-TIN alloy and were available in various oversizes.

The crankcase, cylinder barrels, and cylinder heads were constructed in light alloy, and the heads were each retained by four long and two short studs passing through the cylinders and screwing into the crankcases. Oil tightness was ensured by a paper cylinder base gasket and six cylinder head bolt O-rings per cylinder. The cylinder head gasket was a thick car-type sandwich. Each exhaust port was threaded in the alloy to receive a matching screwed nut retaining

the exhaust pipe, while the inlet had separate stubs. These were bolted in place with a heat-resistant gasket and a trio of Allen screws, ready to receive one of the pair of Dell'Orto SS1–29 carburettors.

Easy access to the valve gear on each side was provided by a large alloy rocker cover, which was retained by eight Allen screws and a one-piece gasket. Underneath this cover, a cast-iron one-piece detachable support held each pair of rockers in place. The tappets were of the simple adjuster screw and lock-nut variety. The valves were inclined at 70 degrees, and a 34.6mm exhaust and 38.6mm inlet were fitted. They employed single coil springs and were seated on special cast-iron inserts.

The camshaft was centrally located in the crutch of the vee between the cylinders, and the base of each pushrod located on a tappet which ran on the appropriate camshaft lobe. The front of the camshaft was connected to the large upper timing gear, part of a matched train of three helical cut steel gears for the timing and oil-pump drive, housed in the timing chest at the front of the engine. The other end of the camshaft incorporated a worm gear to drive the Marelli automobile-type distributor located at the rear base of the offside cylinder.

Engine lubrication was looked after by a 3-litre (6-pint) heavily finned, detachable wet sump which acted as an oil tank, and the gear-type pump housed in the base of the timing chest on the nearside and driven by the lowest of the three gears, which connected to the central crankshaft timing pinion. The oil pump itself comprised a pair of gears, housed in an alloy body. Pressure in the lubrication system was maintained at a constant level by the oil pressure release valve fitted inside the crankcase on the section which supported the sump.

The oil pump drew a steady supply of lubricant from the sump, which after passing through a wire gauze strainer, delivered the oil through ducts into the crankcase. These ducts supplied the oil under pressure to the main bearings, the camshaft housings and the camshaft, through which it passed to lubricate the big-end bearings. Oil passing out around the big-ends was flung out to lubricate the cylinder walls and the remainder of the engine by splash. The cylinder heads received their own, separate supply through external oil pipes.

The big Guzzi's transmission system was closer to automobile practice, rather than that of a conventional motorcycle. Securely bolted to the rear of the crankshaft with six screws was a large-diameter flywheel which doubled as the housing for the dry clutch. This consisted of two friction and two plain plates and eight springs. The clutch assembly was retained inside the flywheel by the electric starter ring gear, which in turn was held in position by eight bolts and spring washers. Passing through the centre of the clutch shaft was a single long clutch pushrod, which then passed through the input shaft of the gearbox to exit behind the clutch operating lever on the rear of the gearbox.

The gearbox housing was bolted on to the rear of the crankcase. This incorporated four speeds and was of the constant mesh, frontal engagement type. The mainshaft was driven by the driving gear on the clutch shaft. All four gears were fixed to the mainshaft, which was a one-piece assembly. The long shaft was provided with four separate engagement gears, two sliding sleeves and also carried the speedometer drive gear.

Rear drive was by Cardan shaft and bevel gears. This took its drive from the rear of the gearbox, via splines on the end of the gearbox layshaft which connected to a universal joint running in a ball race housed in the end of the swinging arm. The exposed portion between the swinging arm and the rear of the gearbox was protected by a rubber gaiter to accommodate the suspension movement. Inside the swinging arm, the universal joint mated up with the drive-shaft, which ran in a pair of ball races, one at each end. At the rear, this was splined to the bevel drive pinion inside the rear drive box, an aluminium casting filled with EP90 oil to lubricate the drive. The crown wheel was meshed directly with the pinion, and mated up with the rear wheel through an internally toothed sleeve in the rear hub. The rear wheel could be removed without the need to disturb the drive, simply by removing the wheel spindle and spacer which kept the wheel centred and in mesh.

The V7 benefited from a decent (by Italian standards, fantastic) 12-volt electrical system, based around a 300-watt Marelli DN62N generator located on the top of the engine between the cylinders in front of the oil breather box and driven from the crankshaft by two pulleys and a rubber belt.

The generator charged a massive 32-amp/hour battery, needed mainly because no kickstarter was fitted and it was very unusual at the time for a bike to rely entirely on its electric starter. The starter was a Marelli MT40H motor, a four-pole design with an output of 0.7 hp and rotating clockwise. It was mounted on the nearside of the crankcase, engaging with the flywheel ring gear via a Marelli IE13DA solenoid fitted directly below the starter motor.

Ignition was again courtesy of Marelli, with an S123A distributor that housed a single set of points and condenser. This was driven by a worm on the camshaft and provided sparks via a single Marelli or Bosch ignition coil. Illumination was provided by a 168mm CEV headlamp, with an oblong alloy bodied rear lamp from the same source.

Like the rest of the specification, the running gear also showed its government-backed heritage with a heavy-duty duplex cradle frame of tubular steel and equally robust swinging arm. The front forks were of the fully enclosed type, but the rear suspension units (unlike those of the military/police version) featured exposed springs. In the braking department massive full-width 220mm drums were specified, with a twin-leading-shoe layout at the front. Unfortunately these brakes were to prove one of the very few weak points of the whole machine, as they were simply not up to the task of effectively retarding the progress of the 234 kg (516 lb) machine. The hubs were built on to 18in Borrani welled alloy rims which carried 4.00 section tyres.

The balance of the cycle parts was conventional and convenient, including the large-capacity 20-litre (4½-gallon) fuel tank and supremely comfortable dual-seat.

The 1968 model year saw a number of changes. These included a new starter motor and square slide Dell'Orto VHB carburettors (still 29mm).

Judged as a touring bike the V7 was (except for its poor braking) an excellent machine; but do not expect it to have any pretension of a sportster – for you will be sorely disappointed.

## V7 Special/Ambassador

In 1969 Guzzi (now with Ing. Lino Tonti as Chief Designer, as Carcano had retired) came out with an enlarged model named the V7 Special. The most notable change was that the engine capacity had increased to 757.486cc, achieved by boring out the cylinders to 83mm; the stroke remained unaltered at 70mm.

A new type of piston was fitted. Still of the four-ring type, the second oil scraper was moved from the original position below the gudgeon pin, up to join the other three above the gudgeon pin, and the skirt was relieved to provide an almost semi-slipper appearance. Pistons were still coded A, B and C. The balance of the engine was altered very little. However, the valves were increased in diameter to 36mm exhaust and 41mm inlet; and they gained small internal valve springs inside the main coils. The clutch springs were also beefed up, whilst new ratios in the rear drive box provided a revised gear of 4.375:1. Engine oil pressure was also upped.

The 'Special' was marketed in the USA as the Ambassador, but except for legal requirements such as a sealed beam headlamp and side reflectors, the Special and Ambassador were the same bike.

## 850GT Eldorado and GT California

First 703cc, then 757cc and finally in late 1971 came a nominal 850 – actually 844.06cc. As the motor was already well oversquare, this time Ing. Tonti opted to increase the stroke to 78mm. Although the bore remained unchanged at 83mm, new 3-ring pistons were employed, with a 9.2:1 compression ratio. The remainder of the engine was much as before, with only a few very minor improvements. Power was increased to 50 bhp. Besides the increase in capacity the transmission had been given an extra gear, making the '850' (and the V7 Sport) the first roadster Guzzis to sport 5-speed gearboxes.

The 850GT (Eldorado in the USA) was essentially, except for its larger engine and five speeds, the same as the V7 Special/Ambassador. It is worth noting that some USA spec Eldorado had the V7 Sport 4-leading shoe front brake. The California package was much more striking, although not a completely 'new' bike, as it used many of the standard Guzzi components in its construction. Moreover it was an early attempt to emulate the American custom-cruiser-type machine. Even the name was clearly chosen to convey the excitement and brashness of the Stateside west coast.

This original 'Cali' model was essentially an 850GT with a number of accessories to provide a full-dress style. These consisted of a large, four-point, toughened perspex screen, laid-back high and wide bars, a high black and white custom seat adorned with a chrome-plated rail, rear carrier, fibre-glass panniers, front and rear crashbars, plus footboards instead of footrests for the rider. The deeply valanced mudguards were the same as on the GT, but chrome-plated rather than simply painted.

V7 Special (Ambassador in America) far away from home in Victoria, Western Australia. Essentially the same as the V7, but with a capacity of 757cc and slight styling changes. It was manufactured between 1969 and 1971.

The engine of the V7. The V7 Special series and the 850GT featured a belt-driven dynamo atop the crankcase. It can be readily identified by the very tall timing cover at the front of engine.

The magnificent 850GT (Eldorado in the USA). The version shown here was offered in 1972-73.

Both models remained unchanged until 1974, when they received a single 300mm cast-iron disc operated by a Brembo caliper mounted at the front of the offside fork leg. Very few of the disc brake models reached the American market. The only other change was the fitment of direction indicators. At the end of that year production ceased in favour of the new 850T model (see Chapter 10).

## V7 Sport

In 1970, after a series of successful record attempts using modified V7s, Ing. Tonti applied his engineering skills to the task of creating an improved version of the 90-degree V-twin, one which was lower, leaner, significantly faster and with better handling. The result was the V7 Sport, the forerunner of all the V-twin Guzzis since that time.

Tonti's first problem was the height of the V-twin engine between the cylinders. This was due to the position occupied by the belt-driven generator at the top of the crankcase, reflected in the very tall timing cover casting at the front.

This particular difficulty was overcome by substituting the top-mounted generator by a German Bosch G1(R) 14V 13A 19 alternator carried directly on the front of the crankshaft. With a new circular timing cover, this greatly reduced the height between the cylinders, allowing the whole machine to be reconstructed into a lower, lighter and therefore more compact motorcycle.

With the height problem overcome a new frame was designed, which was both easy on the eye and effective out on the street. Perhaps the best recommendation of this is the fact that it's still being used today, some 20 years later. With this came new suspension; the front forks (V7 Sport and all Guzzis until Le Mans III and SPNT had 35mm stanchions), of Guzzi's own design, featured sealed dampers, enclosed springs and chrome-plated stanchions.

Probably to take advantage of the Formula 750 racing rules, the engine capacity was changed to 748.8cc. This was effected by reducing the bore size of the 757cc motor down to 82.5mm, while the stroke remained untouched at 70mm. Higher compression 9.8:1 pistons (of the four-ring type) were fitted, while a hotter camshaft, paired coil valve springs and 30mm Dell'Orto carburettors allowed the engine to develop a healthy 52 bhp at the higher 6300 rpm – and this was measured at the rear wheel and was

The 1974 California. It was based around the GT850, but the styling was very much from the West coast of the USA. Both the California and GT850 sported this Brembo disc front brake in their final year of production, in an attempt to improve braking power.

Moto Guzzi's chief designer, Ing. Lino Tonti, worked a miracle in creating the low-line V7 Sport from the original over-fat V7 touring model. It was built from 1972 until early 1974 and formed the basis of all later Guzzi V-twins.

Double-sided, four-leading-shoe front stopper from the V7 Sport – it was much improved over the weak single-sided two-leading-shoe affair on the touring models.

not an optimistic crankshaft reading.

The V7 Sport's drive train employed a mix of components from the 703, 757 and 844cc models. As on the 850GT/California (announced at the same time), the sportster benefited from a 5-speed box. And as with the earlier versions of the V7, the gears were helically cut, mainly in the interest of quieter operation.

Guzzi's V-twin sportster was announced at the same Milan Show in November 1971 as the 850GT and California. Its low centre of gravity (and low seat height), together with sleek, aggressive lines ensured an enthusiastic welcome. Not only this, but its colour scheme was different – an eye-catching metallic lime green for the superbly sculpted 22.5-litre (5-gallon) fuel tank, and triangular side panels. The double cradle frame was in a contrasting Italian racing red, (a total of only 150 were produced in this colour scheme). This combined with a mass of brightwork from sparkling chrome and polished stainless steel items created a true classic amongst large-capacity road-burners of the early 1970s.

With such a low frame, accessibility might have been compromised, but not on the V7 Sport. On the Guzzi, Ing. Tonti had ensured that maintenance would still be straightforward by providing the new frame with fully-detachable bottom rails, a feature which has been continued on subsequent models.

All European spec V7 Sports had right-hand gearchange. There were chrome silencers with slashed ends and 'shark' grilles near the tail. Although the 220mm drum brakes were continued, the front was now double-sided, with four-leading-shoe operation. This finally cured the previously poor braking performance experienced on the touring models. Lighter weight also played its part.

One of the best-liked parts of the V7 Sport's specifications was its swan-neck clip-on handlebars, which could be adjusted both fore and aft and up and down. This allowed an unequalled variation in rider stance for what after all was intended as a sports machine. All USA specification bikes had electric fuel taps as standard equipment. The maximum speed was around the 120 mph mark, which in its day was highly competitive for a 750 twin with full roadgoing equipment. Production commenced in early 1972 and lasted for two years before being superseded for the 1974 model year by the 750 S. The only real change during this time was the colour scheme, and there were various combinations, including burgundy/silver, green/black and red/black. There were however differences for the American market. The V7 Sport remained for 1974 (no 750 S models were imported into the States). So some late 1973 and all 1974 model-year V7 Sports sold to the American importer featured a left-hand gearchange. In addition some late models had a timing chain, dual front discs and a 750 S style bum-stop saddle.

## 750 S

For 1974 the V7 Sport was replaced by the 750 S. Although clearly based around the original sportster, the newer bike had both styling and engineering differences. But the only real engine development was the change from gear drive in the timing case to the use of the much cheaper method of timing chain and sprockets. This system was to be employed on all Guzzi V-twins which came afterwards. The most significant modification to the running gear was the replacement of the huge 220mm double drum front stopper with a pair of hydraulically operated 300mm cast-iron brake discs of Brembo manufacture.

Other new features included a left-hand gearchange operation for European as well as American riders, larger side panels (from the 850 T model), a new design of seat (with room for 1½ people and incorporating a 'bum stop'), and all-new colour schemes (a choice of three) and motifs. There was also the choice of Aprilia direction indicators as a factory-fitted option at extra cost. Another change was to the silencers, which were now finished in matt black, rather than bright chrome plate. As for performance, this was on a par with the V7 Sport with an ability to nudge a genuine 120 mph. The 750 S was not imported into the North American market.

## 750 S3

The final variant of the 750 sports line was the S3, launched at the same time as the touring 850 T3, in early 1975. And although the S3 *looked* like the 750 S at a glance, it actually shared far more, at least mechanically, with the T3. Except for the cylinder barrels, pistons, carburettors/manifolds, crankshaft and clutch flywheel the whole engine/gearbox/clutch assembly was straight from the T3. The cylinder heads were T3 castings, which meant that a major difference between the S3 and its earlier brothers was that the exhaust pipes used bolt-up clamps rather than screwed ring nuts. However the exhaust pipe shape followed the earlier curved type fo the V7 Sport/750 S, not the 'squared' bends of the 850 T/T3.

The 1974 750 S, identified by its double hydraulically operated Brembo discs at the front, 'bum-stop' saddle, black silencers and larger side panels. It also had a timing chain rather than gears as on the V7 Sport.

The next step was the 750 S3. This was a combination of the 750S (frame, exhaust and engine) and the touring 850 T3 (linked brakes, instrument console, side panels, crashbar). It was the last of the true 750 sports models.

The engine of the 750 S3, showing the cylinder and barrel assembly, carburettor and starter motor/solenoid to advantage. The last S3s were built in 1976.

The 750 S3 also shared another feature from the 850 T. Both had no proper air filter element, just a large rubber hose connecting the two carburettors, which led to press reports of 'loud induction noise' louder in practice than any mechanical sound; conventional clip-ons replaced the lovely swan neck variety found on the 750 S. The headlamp shell was changed to black-painted steel.

If anything, maximum speed was *lower* than that of either the V7 Sport or 750 S. In a 1975 *Motor Cycle* road test almost 116 mph was the most the tester could get through the electronic eye. Other features of the S3 were its triple hydraulically operated disc brakes featuring Guzzi's patented linked system (described in the following chapter), T3-type side panels, front crashbars and 170mm Aprilia headlamp. Both petrol taps were of the conventional lever-action type.

The 750 S3 continued to be available until the autumn of 1976, running for a time alongside its replacement, the new 850 Le Mans. As with the 750 S before it, the 750 S3 was not sold across the Atlantic.

**What to look for**

The early Guzzi V-twins featured in this chapter were the best *made* of the whole series. This was because they were generally evolved before the De Tomaso 'maximum profit for minimum outlay' regime had gained full control of the factory's production methods. However, this is not to say that they are without fault, and in fairness to later models the early vees were overweight (especially the V7 the Special, Ambassador and Eldorado) and less powerful. A particular point to check are the exhaust ports. The threaded securing rings can chatter in the head, ruining the thread. The touring models have a strictly limited performance. For example, *Cycle World* in their January 1968 road test of a V7 recorded a maximum speed of only 98 mph, and covered the standing ¼-mile in 16.31 seconds (a terminal speed of 81.15 mph).

Spares will also be a problem, as they are often different from later bikes, particularly cycle parts such as swan neck clip-ons and 'shark grille' silencers from the V7 Sport and 750 S. Braking on the touring bikes is another less than satisfactory feature – do *not* expect modern standards.

However, all possess a certain charm and they are certainly far more robust than virtually any other Italian bike of their era. The shaft final drive is another bonus. A warning though: make sure the final drive is fully serviceable, as it will be expensive to put right.

Watch out for ex-government V7 models sold off as civilian models – a more common practice than you may think.

**Star rating: V7 Sport five deserved stars, 750 S four stars, V7 series touring models plus 750 S3 three stars, California two stars.**
The V7 Sport is without doubt right up there with bikes such as the Ducati 750 SS, Laverda SFC and MV Agusta 750S as a true classic Italian sportster of the early 1970s. And its appeal and value are set to rise even higher in the next few years, hence its full five-star treatment. The 750 S is almost as nice, but not quite, spoilt by its cheap and nasty timing chain instead of the more expensive gears, 'easy-rust' black silencers and hydraulic double discs in place of that unique double-sided drum front brake. Middle-of-the-road three stars are given to the V7 touring bikes and the 750 S3, all of which are not quite as good as they should be; the V7s because of their obsolete looks; the S3 because it is related more to the 850 T3 than the original V7 Sport/750 S. With the S3 it really is a case of 'looks can deceive'.

As for the California, this is essentially a customized, chrome-plated, poser bike for those who like the West Coast American style. This limits its appeal and therefore is the reason it only gets a two-star rating. Do not confuse this with the later 'Cali' models with the lower frame and alternator electrics. Of all the early Guzzi vees the rare green and red V7 Sport commands the highest premium. But make sure all the cycle parts are there, as some of them are difficult to find.

**Summary**
None of the early Guzzi V-twins will really disappoint. They also have a special class, which the later bikes never quite achieved. *Cycle World* put it nicely: 'The dyed-in-the-wool touring motorcyclist will find the Moto Guzzi V7 a delight to own. His motorcycling cronies will find it an everlasting source of envy. The Moto Guzzi is one of a very small number of motorcycles that can create a great deal of noise, while remaining very smooth, very quiet.'

# CHAPTER 10

# T Series

| | | |
|---|---|---|
| ** | 850 T | 1974-75 |
| *** | 850 T3 | 1975-82 |
| *** | 850 T4 | 1980-83 |
| ** | 850 T5 | 1983-85 |

## History

A landmark in the evolution of the large-capacity touring Guzzi V-twin was the 850 T, a machine which ushered in a whole new image and sales potential for the Mandello del Lario big vees. Until then you could either buy a sportster with sweet handling and nimble lines or a supremely comfortable but decidedly overweight cruiser – but not a machine that combined the virtues of both. The 850 T changed all this at a stroke, providing potential customers with a *sports/tourer* in a single machine. So began the T series, bikes which provided a sensible, if not particularly glamorous, middle-of-the-road approach and ran for over a decade from the mid-1970s to the mid-1980s.

## 850 T

In reality the 850 T owed far more to the V7 Sport than to the V7 touring models. It not only employed the Sport's chassis and suspension, but it also featured much of the engine design and general specification of the 750 S, a new development of the V7 Sport, which had gone on sale early in 1974.

In fact the 850 T and 750 S shared a number of features. These included the adoption of a hydraulic disc front brake with a Brembo caliper (in fact the 750 S had twin hydraulic discs), 30mm Dell'Orto VHB carburettors, Bosch 180-watt alternator, stainless steel mudguards (although of a different design)

and a drum rear brake.

The 850 T and 750 S engines were also the last of the Guzzi V-twins to employ the dated wire-mesh oil filtration system introduced on the original V7. It is worth noting that the final batch of 850 Ts, constructed just before production ceased in late 1974, were fitted with the much improved car-type canister oil filter designed for the T3 and 750 S3 engines and which required a new sump.

Externally the obvious difference between the 850 T's engine and those fitted to the earlier touring models was the replacement of the belt-driven Marelli generator. Previously, the position of this atop the crankcase between the cylinder barrels had meant that the front of the engine was dominated by a tall alloy outer casing. Now, like the sportsters, the 850 T used a much neater Bosch alternator mounted on the front of the crankshaft.

Much of the balance of the electrical components were also of Bosch manufacture, so bringing the 850 T into line with the 750 S. The exceptions were the lighting equipment (a mixture of Aprilia and CEV), the Marelli distributor and twin ignition coils, plus the switchgear.

A feature of the machine was its excellent riding position and well-padded dual-seat, allowing long distances to be covered without the need to get off and exercise tired muscles. A large-capacity, 25-litre petrol tank

The first of the T Series, the 850T was introduced during mid-1974. Although it shared the same capacity as the earlier GT model, it employed the chassis from the 750 V Sport and 750 S, together with the crankshaft-mounted alternator.

combined with excellent fuel economy (60 mpg under touring conditions being within reach) ensured that the bike's long-distance touring ability could be explored to the full.

In the engine department it used the larger-capacity bore and stroke dimensions developed for the 850 GT/California. But its specification was different in several vital respects. The chrome-plated cylinder bores carried higher compression 9.5:1 pistons, while the camshaft profile was that of the 750 S. Once again, in traditional Guzzi V-twin practice the piston and barrel assemblies were coded A, B or C, with crankshafts and con-rods colour-coded either white or blue. Power output was 53 bhp at 6000 rpm. Together with a greatly improved power-to-weight ratio over the earlier touring models, the 850 T was capable of 115-118 mph, depending on the conditions and the weight of the rider.

Unlike any of the other T-series models, the 850 T had lockable side panels, a metal front brake master cylinder cap, drum rear brake and a metal-foil material for the stripes on the tank and side panels.

Whilst the 850 T was a clever marriage of a soft large-capacity engine and sports bike handling, it was still a flawed design due to its poor braking performance. A particular deficiency was the single front disc, which felt wooden in operation and lacked sufficient power to stop the machine really effectively. The only answer was either to fit a second disc, or better still buy the bike which replaced it, the 850 T3. As for colour schemes, the 850 T came in a choice of salmon, brown or metallic green. Only the last two were offered in the USA.

### 850 T3

The biggest difference (and improvement) between the 850 T and the 850 T3 was its braking. The latter bike was the first Guzzi to feature the now famous Integral Braking System. This has a triple disc system with double front discs, and single rear disc layout. The disc material is cast iron, eliminating the pause in wet conditions experienced with the stainless steel variety.

The integral brake system is operated by the foot pedal, and the pressure on this pedal operates the brakes pads on the rear and one front disc (the left). This system automatically produces the correct amount of power for maximum braking efficiency, to the front and rear wheels, and removes the responsibility from the rider to co-ordinate hand and foot pressures. This means that in normal braking conditions the machine will maintain its natural line, without the rear or front of the machine breaking adhesion with the road surface, eliminating the possibility of dangerous skidding. The aforementioned is for a dry tarmac road in serviceable condition. The Guzzi system does not perform so well as the latest ABS system in poor weather such as rain or snow. However, that said, it is entirely possible to brake from high speed with both hands removed from the handlebars (on a dry road) in a perfectly straight line to almost zero mph. Disc

Next in the line was the 850 T3, with Guzzi's patented linked braking system. The foot pedal operated the rear and nearside front disc. A handlebar-mounted lever controlled the other front disc. Launched in early 1975, the T3 went on sale in Britain during May of that year.

The master cylinder for the foot-operated linked brake system on the 850 T3, situated behind the right-hand side panel. Also note the electrical components, including the fuse box and flasher relay.

Dual cast iron discs and Brembo calipers.

Bevel-drive box, three-way adjustable shocks and seamed Lafranconi silencer from T3.

diameters on the T3 were: front 300mm, rear 242mm.

Other changes, although less noticeable, were none-the-less important in their own way. Design improvements had taken place to both the oil and air filtration systems. The former had the disposable car-type oil filter as used on the final batch of 850 Ts, while for first time on a Guzzi V-twin the carbs had a proper air filter. This was a disposable paper cartridge which provided the engine with additional protection, particularly the chrome-plated cylinder bores.

The output of the Bosch alternator had been increased to 280 watts. The warning lights and Veglia instruments were now housed in a plastic console in place of the previous alloy component, whilst the ignition switch had three, rather than four, positions. The handlebars had a higher rise than before and the clutch cable incorporated a cut-out switch, preventing

the engine being started without the clutch lever being pulled in. (This was a precaution against the rider starting the bike whilst in gear.)

Out on the street the T3 offered a similar performance to the 850 T, but it was a better balanced machine, thanks to its much improved braking capabilities.

But every motorcycle has its downside, and on the T3 it was the finish. The paintwork and chromework fell far short of the standards of the earlier models. In addition the rubber components had a nasty habit of rotting or prematurely failing in service. The latter is best noted for leaking front forks, gearbox drive-shafts and hub oil seals. Other problem areas included rusting discs, failed universal joints and weak switchgear.

For all these apparent faults the T3 is still a fine motorcycle. It's well balanced with comfort, safe handling and excellent

From the 1979 model year, the T3 sported cast alloy wheels, CEV headlamp and indicators, SP-type seat and Le Mans II rear light.

braking. A good all-rounder in fact. Practical rather than glamorous – for riding, not posing.

The T3's only real update came in 1979 when several cosmetic changes were introduced. The most noteworthy was the introduction of cast alloy wheels of the design already in use on certain other models, including the Le Mans and SP (Spada in Britain). The later, oblong rear light from these two machines was now specified for the T3, along with the SP-type seat, a lockable fuel cap, CEV headlamp (with a black shell), SP-type switchgear, CEV indicators, an improved centre-stand and a black plastic alternator cover. However, the mechanics remained unaltered, a testimony to the basic soundness of the design. There were lots of colour options, but the US market only got black or silver, with gold or white pinstripes.

## 850 T4

The following year, 1980, the T3 became the T4, but just to confuse matters Guzzi continued production of the original T3, mainly because of demand in certain export markets and for police/military sales. And the T4 was not imported into the USA.

The T4 was not just a follow-on from the T3, but also virtually an economy version of the SP NT (see Chapter 13), albeit with a smaller power plant. The 844cc engine was that of the T3, but with Nickasil plated bores instead of the chrome finish which had been employed since the 850 capacity size had been introduced. The silencers were SP NT components and the T4 had the considerable benefit of having the SP handlebar fairing (but not the leg shields) as standard equipment, together with an SP NT dual-seat. The centre-stand, again from the SP, was much simpler to operate, and the T4's specification was completed with SP rear indicators to match those of the fairing, and the front brake calipers repositioned behind, rather than in front, of the fork sliders.

Introduced in 1980, the 850 T4 featured several changes. These included an SP-type handlebar fairing (but without the legshields), V1000/SPNT seat, new silencers and Nickasil-coated cylinder bores instead of the chrome-plated type which had been used on the 850 series since its inception.

Only one colour scheme was offered. This was a deep non-metallic wine-red with gold lining for the tank, side panels and fairing. The frame and stands, swinging arm and rear light support/number plate holder were in black, with silver wheels and fork sliders. Almost what one would have found on any number of British bikes of the 1950s.

## T5

The final development of the T series was the T5. Launched in the spring of 1983 it was largely the work of the new De Tomaso-inspired styling syndicate in Modena, rather than Guzzi's own team back at Mandello. Unfortunately this body of so-called experts may well have been just that when it came to four wheels, but their offering for bike enthusiasts proved a sales disaster.

The T5 was a mixture of components, some from the T3/4, some from the Le Mans III, some from the new V75, some from the

SPII (although in fact the SPII arrived after the T5) and others, individual to the T5.

The basic mechanics came from the T3/4; the 'square' cylinders, heads and rocker covers (but not the carbs) from the Le Mans III; the fairing from the V75; controls, instruments, seat side-panels, tank, front mudguard and front wheel assembly from the SPII.

Like the V35 Imola II, V50 Monza II and V65 Lario, the original T5 was unique amongst modern Guzzis in having 16 in front *and* rear wheels. This would appear to have been a poorly thought-out attempt to 'modernize', as ground clearance for the likes of the silencers, footrests and pedals was not sufficient. Because of this Guzzi were forced to bring in a modified version for the 1985 season with a larger 18 in rear wheel. This at least solved the matter of the ground clearance, although handling and road holding were never up to the standard of the

The 1985 850 T5. Changes from the earlier version (débuted in 1983) were an 18in rear wheel (formerly 16in), modified screen, tank, carburettors and colour scheme. Sales never matched expectations.

earlier T models. This was a great pity, because in several other areas the T5 was a competent motorcycle. And certainly the choice of 16 in wheels did not affect the handling so badly as it did with the Le Mans IV and SPII; the latter machines – with their greater performance – were most unsettling.

Even with the substitution of the 18 in rear wheel, sales of the T5 did not improve, and the model was discontinued at the end of 1985.

### What to look for

All the T series are everyday workhorses rather than exotic weekend showbikes. Therefore mileages are likely to be high and it is vitally important to make an extra effort when checking over the machine prior to purchase.

Areas to check thoroughly include electrical components, particularly switches; the front engine mounting bolt which can become seized; hydraulic brake components such as discs, calipers and master cylinders; universal joints; front forks (the damper

units and oil seals); rotting seat pan and rotting silencers. These sounds like a disaster, but a bonus is that the engine, gearbox and clutch tend to give very little trouble, provided they receive a reasonable amount of regular maintenance. Even if they do not, that lumbering V-twin motor seems to run longer than most.

### Star rating: 850 T3 and T4 three solid stars; 850 T and T5 basically sound, but with design deficiencies, so only two stars

Middle-of-the-road three stars for 850 T3 and T4. Both are sound designs which are well suited to their intended role as everyday transport and touring motorcycles. They will never be the target of collectors, but are a good bet if you want to ride rather than show your machine. But make sure you find an example which has been well cared for, as there are lots of rough ones about. As for the 850 T/T5 models, these are still worth considering provided you accept their drawbacks: 850 T brakes, 850 T5 handling/ground clearance.

CHAPTER 11

# Le Mans

| | | |
|---|---|---|
| ***** | Le Mans I | 1976-78 |
| **** | Le Mans II | 1978-80 |
| **** | Le Mans III | 1981-84 |
| **** | Le Mans IV | 1984- |

**History**
During the last 20 years one Guzzi model has stood head and shoulders above the rest: the Le Mans. Named after the famous French racing circuit, the Guzzi Le Mans has proved to be one of the classics of the Italian post-war motorcycling scene and it has been built in larger numbers and over a longer period than any other large-capacity Mandello V-twin.

Originally conceived to compete with rivals such as the Ducati 900SS, Laverda 3C and MV Agusta America of the mid-1970s, it is still in production, albeit in Mark IV form, in the 1990s.

A prototype machine was tested in the 1973 Barcelona 24 hours marathon. Ridden by Riva/Gazzola it came home fifth.

**Mark I**
Technically, the new sportster, which was announced at the Milan Show in November 1975 and went on sale the following spring, drew heavily from both the 750 S3 and 850 T3. In fact, the engine assembly and transmission was essentially only a tuned version of the 'cooking' 850 with identical cylinder dimensions, gearbox and final drive. To achieve the extra zip needed in its new role, the Le Mans (soon given the nickname 'Lemon') had higher compression pistons (10.2:1), larger valves (37mm exhaust, 44mm inlet), a more lumpy cam profile and a pair of 36mm Dell'Orto PHF pumper carburettors with large plastic bellmouths.

At the time of the launch of the Le Mans Mark I it was *claimed* that maximum power output was 81 bhp, providing a top speed of 134 mph. Reality was somewhat different: 71 bhp and 124 mph. Even so, this performance, combined with the Le Mans' surefooted handling, excellent braking and aggressive style, at last provided Guzzi with a motorcycle with which it could take on all-comers in the superbike stakes.

A sporting stance was achieved with clip-ons, rear-set foot controls, a racing-type 'bum-stop' saddle, bikini fairing, drilled discs, matt black frame and exhaust system (both of which were extremely prone to the ravages of rust in more northern climes), and silver cast alloy wheels; every line of the machine stated speed.

Befitting the name and image, the Le Mans was offered in Europe in bright Italian racing red finish (tank, side panels, fairing and mudguards), or alternatively it could be ordered in a metallic light grey/blue (Ice blue) or brilliant white (the latter from March 1977). But it was the red which proved by far the most popular, and it was this finish which, at least in the author's eyes enhanced the Le Mans' sporting image. Stateside the Le Mans were offered in the same colours, but few of the Ice blue were imported.

Original and best – and to many Guzzi fans that is just what the Le Mans I represents. Produced between 1976 and 1978 it is considered a modern classic.

The bike's more civilized aspects were subtly subdued. Although direction indicators were fitted, they and their support arms were finished in black, blending more easily into the contours of the machine than would otherwise have been expected. Pillion footrests were provided, but like many Japanese race replicas of today, it was rather too much of an intimate affair, with the passenger expected to put his or her butt on the padded seat hump.

The seat was a distinctive feature of the Le Mans, and could have been both a stylistic and ergonomic (for one person only) coup. As it was, the seat was to prove one of the most poorly designed components of the whole machine. The interesting feature about this seat was the way in which it was moulded so that the nose extended over the rear of the tank, a curiously effective design item which should have ensured rider comfort. The problem was that the whole structure was moulded in one piece from foam rubber, which simply was not strong enough for the job, with whole chunks of foam actually breaking away, particularly from the poorly supported frontal section. A favourite and practical remedy was to fit a seat from the earlier 750 S3 model. Only the very first few US spec. Mark I's had the 'bum' stop saddle. Most had the flatter MKII saddle, US MKIs featured a fairing which differed from the European type in that the headlamp was extended by way of a 'tube' forward. Other less than satisfactory items included a batch of undersize fork legs which led to leaking fork seals (this was a problem on several other larger Guzzis of the same era), unreliable switchgear (ditto), difficult to operate stands (ditto) and a miserable 12-volt 20-amp battery, compared to the 32-amp hour type fitted on the other V-twin models.

But the worst aspect of the whole machine was its finish – or, more accurately, lack of it. The matt black frame was absolutely awful, as was the similarly finished exhaust system. Both were real rust traps. I have known frames to have been replaced under

The Le Mans I as raced during 1977 by Sports
Motorcycles' director, John Sears.

warranty (something which is normally an extremely rare occurance). These major and minor grumbles apart, the balance of the Le Mans I soon enabled it to build up a particularly loyal and enthusiastic following, for in many ways it was the most practical of all Italian sportsters.

On the credit side there was the undoubted benefit of shaft final drive; but there were also such worthwhile features as steering head and rear-fork pivot on taper roller bearings, screws and locknuts for tappet adjustment, easy maintenance thanks to a basically simple design, good-quality Allen bolts on engine and gearbox assembly, dual-stand springs, easy to operate fuel taps, bolted-on protector plates to keep boots off

silencers, a footbrake pedal adjustable for height and a strong steering lock. Finally there was an efficient (and easy to use) manual steering damper.

Thanks to a wide spread of power and relatively soft foam rubber saddle the Le Mans I made quite a good long-distance bike. Fuel consumption was between 50-60 mpg depending on riding style, which compared well with contemporary opposition. Many consider the original version the prettiest of all the Le Mans models.

## Mark II

Even though the Le Mans had proved to be a consistent top-seller in its V-twin range, Guzzi decided in early 1978 that it was time to consider an 'updating' exercise. The result of this appeared in time to make its début in September that year at the massive biennial Cologne Show in West Germany.

Known as the Le Mans II (the original had been uncoded), the most obvious change was the adoption of an SP-style three-piece full fairing (but with an oblong headlamp unit) which endowed the whole bike with a much more angular look. At the same time the Le Mans had gained most of the fairing-mounted equipment from the SP. This comprised the complete instrument layout and switchgear, including the quartz clock and voltmeter. The large, moulded rubber dashboard was suitably re-inscribed 'Le Mans'. The front indicators were now integral with the fairing, and the clip-on bars were changed to suit the fairing's upper section.

The red finish was as before, except that there was now more of it thanks to that fairing – and the frame continued in the rust-prone matt black finish. But the metallic blue/grey and white were deleted and a royal blue became the other option.

Many observers (and quite a few members of the press) initially reported that the power output had been raised and that the exhaust system had been redesigned – both were untrue.

There were changes, and two of these removed earlier shortcomings. The troublesome single saddle had already been replaced during 1977 for one which provided not only a true two-up capability, but did not fall apart, even though it was constructed from an almost identical material. And although the very first Le Mans IIs retained the old-type battery, this was very soon replaced by a beefier 32-amp hour component.

There were several other more minor

The Le Mans II employed an SP-derived fairing and a more angular style. Performance was largely unchanged.

'Cockpit' of the Le Mans II. Instruments, left to right: clock, tachometer, speedometer and voltmeter.

changes. Amongst these, the front brake calipers were relocated at the rear of the fork legs, which were now finished in black rather than silver. The ignition switch and rear brake master cylinder cap had been changed for the improved SP type, the latter linked to an idiot light when the fluid level dropped too low; and finally the hand-operated friction-type steering damper was replaced by a hydraulic unit of a totally different design and operation. The last modification brought about the following comment from *Motorcycle Sport* during their November 1980 road test of a MkII: 'The steering damper control can no longer be varied on the move, and a fine-thread adjuster is fiddly, so altering the degree of 'bite' is a long-winded job. Furthermore, short of disconnecting it altogether the damper cannot be neutralized; the first type could.'

Out on the street, the paper performance of the fully faired Le Mans is not noticeably different from the original. The now defunct British magazine *Motorcycling* recorded a maximum (rider prone) speed of almost 127 mph and averaged 48 mpg (including speed testing sessions). Tester Charles Deane complained of poorly designed switchgear, difficult to operate stands and an overfirm dualseat, which he said 'did little to absorb road shocks and lifted only just enough to reach the toolkit below; it also didn't lock'. Overall Deane remained favourably impressed with the Le Mans II, in particular its ability to match many 1000cc bikes of the day in performance and comfortably beat them on fuel economy.

To these comments can be added the final paragraph from the 1980 *Motorcycle Sport* test: 'BMW's best is tantalizing, the big MV beyond reach even secondhand, Laverda's triple very impressive, Ducati's 900 still more attractive, Suzuki's GS1000 a better financial proposition, Honda's CB900F probably the finest value for money of all. But as the prospect of continual chain maintenance on every reasonable alternative is inescapable, I'll take the Guzzi. It is the most satisfying modern large-capacity machine of my experience.'

In late 1980, a number of major modifications were introduced on the Le Mans II. The chrome-plated cylinder bores were superseded by Nickasil ones. The internal sealed fork dampers (which had been prone to premature failure) were modified, and the forks were converted to air-assisted operation. Rear suspension was also changed, with the substitution of Paioli units. In Britain importers Coburn & Hughes offered a 'special edition' in black and gold (at extra cost); this was primarily to shift excess stocks from their warehouse in readiness for a completely new version, the Le Mans III. No Mark IIs were sold in the USA. A special model, the CX1000, was introduced in 1980 and sold through into 1981. This was basically a Mark II chassis, with a 1000cc SP engine.

## Le Mans III

This was no simple cosmetic updating of the Le Mans, but a major redesign. The changes were not simply skin-deep, but internal too, with the engine, in particular, receiving updates. Most noticeable of these were the new, square-finned cylinder heads and matching Nickasil-plated cylinder barrels. Although such fundamentals as the camshaft profile and valve sizes remained unchanged, and even though the compression ratio was actually decreased from 10.2 to 9.8:1 (in the interests of improved low-speed running and torque) the performance was still bettered by a full 3 bhp, while engine torque increased to 7.6kg/m at 6200 rpm.

This was quite an achievement by the Guzzi design team, because it came about purely by the combination of superior machining equipment improving tolerances, the use of aluminium rocker supports (which also helped quieten the tappets) and an improved air filter and exhaust system. The last mentioned component was in fact the first from a European motorcycle to meet the stringent EEC regulation CEE 78.1015. The double-skin exhaust pipes and silencers were now finished in bright chromework.

The fairing was another item to undergo major changes, and the new design (again the result of testing in Guzzi's own wind tunnel) had considerably smaller dimensions than before. There was also a form of spoiler offering deflection of the air current past the base of the fuel tank and the top of the cylinder heads. The instrument console had been completely changed. Pride of place went to a new 100mm white-faced Veglia tachometer. This was flanked by a smaller speedometer on the right, voltmeter on the left and rows of idiot lights below. These, together with the ignition switch, were housed in a thick rubber console, as were the two green indicator lights.

The same 'fire-engine' red and black colour scheme as the Mk II now featured matching red fork sliders. The tank had been enlarged to 25 litres (5.5 gallons) and was reshaped to set off the new squared-off cylinder head and barrel finning. This in turn provided the engine with an almost brutal, squat look. The Mk III was also offered in white and silver, but the latter colour was not available in America.

The seat too was new, not to everyone's liking, and this is what one road tester had to say: 'The seat is as long, narrow and hard as a length of railway track, and it's a long way to the controls, even for a six-footer like me.' One definite improvement was the headlamp, which on the Mk III was a first-class quartz H4 affair, at last making night riding a safe pleasure. The main beam in particular was excellent.

There were many changes on the Le Mans III,
including the new square-finned cylinder heads and
matching Nickasil-plated barrels.

A Le Mans III in the town of Lecco, a few kilometres
from the Guzzi factory in the summer of 1983.

## Mk IV

The next move came in late 1984 with the introduction of the Le Mans 1000 (more commonly known as the Mk IV). Like the V1000, California II and SP models, the Mk IV used the larger 948.8cc (88×78mm) engine, but obviously in a higher state of tune in line with the Le Mans' more sporting role. The valves were both 3mm larger in diameter than on the 850 engine, at 47mm inlet and 40mm exhaust. The compression ratio was upped to 10:1 and the newcomer employed larger 40mm Dell'Ortos and new exhaust pipes of the same diameter. The silencers were also different, and both they and the header and balance pipes were finished in a gloss black chrome. The net result of these technical changes saw the power output rise to 86 bhp at the crankshaft, and maximum speed out on the road go up to 141 mph (which was over 10 mph more than the Mark III).

As for styling, the Mark IV relied heavily on the then current V65 Lario, itself drawing inspiration from the V35 Imola II and V50 Monza II (see Chapter 14). There was even more use of the the main colour (red), including wheels and the bottom, detachable frame tubes. A bellypan was incorporated below the fairing, following the fashion of the mid-1980s, which was very much a case of the Italians following the Japanese rather than the other way around. The Mark IV was also offered in white.

The Le Mans 1000 (unofficially named the Mark IV) arrived in late 1984. It had styling based on the V65 Lario and a 140 mph potential . . .

. . .shame about the decision to fit a 16in front wheel. This spoilt the previous excellent handling characteristics.

This trend was also to be seen in the use of a 16 in front wheel. And what a disastrous move it proved too, as I can well remember from my first ride on the new machine in early 1985. At first I thought the tyre must be punctured, but no, everything was in order, and the vague handling was due entirely to the use of that 16 in wheel – without any other noticeable changes to the frame or suspension. Besides the change to a 120/80 V16 front tyre, Guzzi fitted a wider 130/80

section rear tyre, but this stayed at 18 in. The brakes were still of the patented linked disc system, but were now a uniform 270mm all round.

Fairing and aerofoils were closely related to those of the Le Mans III, except for the front indicators, which were now sharply angular and in fact doubled in a most efficient manner as wind deflectors for the rider's hands. The instrument console was unchanged from the Le Mans III, and was also adopted from the Lario. Different components which the Lario gave to the latest Le Mans included switchgear, foam rubber handlebar grips and dog-leg control levers. Much louder windtone horns replaced the conventional type specified for the earlier marks.

Since it was launched the only major change to the 'Mk IV' came in 1987. This featured several modifications and the introduction of a special edition. The most important change was the replacement of the awful 16 in front wheel by an 18 in component, thereby restoring Guzzi's good name for the safe handling and bend swinging abilities.

The 1987 Le Mans Special Edition had a black-painted engine and transmission, Biturbo dampers in the forks, and a close-ratio gear cluster. Cosmetically a one-off red and white paint job, together with a red seat covering gave it a distinctive appearance.

Many of the Special Edition's imported into the States were damaged in shipment when salt water entered the shipping container. The bikes corroded to various degrees and were sold at reduced prices without warranty.

The 18 in front wheel model did not reach the American market until 1989 where it is known as the 'Mark V'. The latest Le Mans has a frame mounted fairing.

Even though the latest Le Mans has retained much of the original's basic layout and general specification, owners of earlier Marks will quickly point out that it is too Japanese, but put a rider of a large-capacity Oriental bike on board and he will soon tell that this statement is 'a load of rubbish' and that it's still very much a Guzzi.

By 1988 the Le Mans IV had regained an 18in front
wheel and, with it, its handling prowess. The styling
is best described as sharp.

**What to look for**

All versions of the Le Mans enjoy the
advantages of the big Guzzi V-twin as
outlined in earlier Chapters and share its
failures. And usually because it is the most
sporting model in the range (barring the
limited production and very special Doctor
John Replica), this Jekyll and Hyde nature
will be even more distinct.

It is also important to buy an ex-enthusiast
machine which has had loving care lavished
upon it, rather than a cheaper bike which
has been run into the ground. The former
will prove much the better investment in the
long term.

One word of warning, I would advise
potential buyers to make sure the Le Mans IV
has an 18 in, rather than a 16 in front wheel.

**Star rating: Mark I five stars; other versions
four stars**

Many Guzzi buffs consider (rightly in the
author's view) the Mark I to have been the
best of the bunch. It possesses flowing,
contoured lines and a true classic style;
whereas the Mark II and those that followed
have a largely angular outline and sharp
aggressive features, changes in my mind
made by marketing men, rather than
motorcyclists. The original was untouched
by these individuals.

All the Le Mans models have retained a
unique charm and enjoyed pride of
ownership, which is probably why they had
such a long run and are still in production
today.

Mark Revelle in a test of the 850 Mark III
(*Which Bike?*, November 1981) made the
following comment: 'Using the Le Mans to
commute is like keeping an eagle in an
aviary. It is in its element beneath open skies,
where the engine's torque and power can be
fully exploited.' Yes, Mark, this really does
sum things up perfectly.

# CHAPTER 12

# Vertical Twins and Fours

| | | |
|---|---|---|
| *** | 350 GTS Four | 1974-79 |
| *** | 400 GTS Four | 1974-79 |
| **** | 254 Four | 1977-81 |
| * | 125 2C 4T | 1979-83 |

## History

One of the big events of the 1972 motorcycle year was the launch of the prototype Benelli 750 Sei – the world's first production 6-cylinder road bike. This, together with the 4-cylinder 500 Quattro, was the idea of factory boss, De Tomaso, with the design work undertaken by Ing. Aurelio Bertocchi, son of Guerrino Bertocchi, former chief mechanic of the 1950s Maserati Grand Prix car team.

Ing. Bertocchi was also the creator of various other 4-cylinder models of the combined Benelli/Moto Guzzi motorcycle group. These included 250, 350 and 400 versions for Moto Guzzi, plus a 125 twin.

History shows these machines, together with their Benelli brothers, to have been only moderately successful in the showrooms, although in many ways they were trend-setting designs (especially the Benelli 750 six and the Benelli/Moto Guzzi 250 Four). Equally the De Tomaso companies were rightly accused of copying the Japanese (in the shape of the 350, 400 and 500 Fours).

## 350 GTS

At the heart of this, the first Moto Guzzi-badged, Benelli-based, across-the-frame 4-cylinder model was a chain-drive sohc engine, with a capacity of 345.5cc (50×44mm). It featured a five main bearing crankshaft and horizontally split crankcases.

The cylinders were inclined 10 degrees and with a compression ratio of 10:1 Guzzi claimed 38 bhp at 9500 rpm. Carburation was by a quartet of Dell'Orto square slide VHB instruments, with a choke size of 20mm, while lubrication was effected by a trocoid pump, with a replaceable cartridge oil filter located centrally at the front of the crankcase. A wet multi-plate clutch transmitted the power via a 5-speed gearbox and chain final drive to the rear wheel.

Electrical equipment included a 12v 12-amp/hour battery, Bosch alternator and starter motor (although a kickstarter was retained), 170mm chrome headlamp, CEV square rear light and Aprilia indicators. Many of the machine's cycle components, including the Marzocchi forks, Grimeca drum brakes (a 180mm dual unit at the front), tank, seat and side panels were from the 250 TS two-stroke twin of the same era. Even the full duplex frame was very similar to the 250 TS type. Both also shared the same 17-litre fuel tank. All this made the 350 GTS a very compact bike, with a reasonable power-to-weight ratio. Dry weight was 168kg (370 lb).

The first production model appeared in time for the beginning of the 1974 sales season, after making its début in prototype form at the Milan Show late the previous year.

A year after it went on sale the GTS

Moto Guzzi's 350 GTS made its début in 1974. It was closely related to the Benelli 500 Quattro, which itself was an Italian copy of Honda's CB500.

received a facelift with a 300mm cast iron disc and Brembo caliper up front replacing the previous double-sided drum brake; at the same time the Marzocchi front forks were junked in favour of Guzzi's own type with sealed damper units. Other changes introduced at the same time included an oblong instrument console and new graphics for the tank and side panels.

### 400 GTS

Even though production of the original Guzzi middleweight four continued, a larger-capacity version made its bow at the 1975 Milan Show. Going on sale early the following year, the 400 GTS was essentially the same machine as its smaller brother, except for an increase in cubic capacity and '400 GTS' badging. The larger engine size of 397.2cc was achieved by lengthening the

stroke, rather than the bore, from 44 to 50.6mm providing almost square 50×50.6mm dimensions. Maximum power was now 40 bhp at 9500 rpm and top speed was 102 mph. Both the 400 and 350 GTS models remained in production until 1979, but never sold in any great numbers.

### What to look for

Basically blessed with sure-footed handling, efficient braking and sweet-running engines, both the 350 and 400 GTS Fours suffered from mediocre performance and poor finish; the chromework (of which there was plenty) suffered particularly badly. Finally the Basso silencers of the four-into-four exhaust system were prone to rotting in much the same way as the very similar Honda CB500 4-cylinder models.

The engine shows clear Honda ancestry. But cycle parts, including frame and suspension, were typically Italian, as was the sure-footed handling.

## Star rating: three stars – just

The good points (handling, braking and engine smoothness) ensure a middle-of-the-road rating. But only buy one if it has been well cared for. Spares are not likely to prove particularly easy to find.

## 254

In 1976 came the definitive Moto Guzzi across-the-frame four, the jewel-like 254, which did not stand for its capacity, but 'two-fifty four cylinder'. Actually, as with the twin-cylinder two-stroke 250 TS, the 254 had a capacity of only 231.1cc (44×38mm). Unlike the larger fours, the 254 was something

From 1975 the 350 GTS (and the outwardly identical 400 version) were updated with a single Brembo disc front stopper, together with a pair of Guzzi's own front forks – replacing the Grimeca drum brake/Marzocchi forks of the original version.

The world's first series production 4-cylinder 250, the Moto Guzzi 254 (together with its Benelli counterpart). An early example is shown here on display at the Cologne Show in West Germany during September 1976.

which Guzzi (or Benelli) could claim to have been their own work and not pirated from Honda.

With a specification that included 10.1:1 compression pistons, 27.8 bhp at 11,500 rpm, a quartet of 18mm Dell'Orto carburettors, a 5-speed close-ratio gearbox, electric starter with 12-volt 12-amp/hour battery and alternator, plus dinky 12-spoke cast alloy wheels, a 260mm hydraulically operated Brembo front disc brake and a dry weight of only 117kg (258 lb), the 254 seemed to offer potential customers the perfect quarter-litre street bike.

But there were two considerable problems. One was the weird styling job, which contrasted sharply with the conservative appearance of the 350 and 400 GTS models and, perhaps most harmful of all, a sky-high price tag. In the author's opinion, both these failings would have disappeared if the tiny four had been dressed as a race replica, with a four-into-four exhaust (instead of the four-into-two), clip-ons, maybe a fairing, plus more conventionally mounted instruments.

As it was the stylist created something which just did not mix. For all its advanced specification the speedo, tacho, warning lights and ignition switch were mounted within a tank-top panel, *vintage* style. And by using a single silencer on each side of the bike it was not instantly recognizable that the 254 had four cylinders; instead it gave the impression of being a commonplace twin. Even the square-edged tank, side panels, seat base and mudguards did less than justice to the unique nature of the machine. But underneath lurked a heart of gold, and one, together with its Benelli stablemate, that is highly prized by collectors around the world today.

The factory claimed a maximum speed of 99 mph, which was highly respectable for its time, although totally outclassed by today's sports 250s, such as the KR1S, RGV or TZR. Even so the Guzzi/Benelli design is still the only 4-cylinder machine of its engine size to reach full-scale production and to have been sold on a worldwide basis.

**What to look for**
For markets such as the UK, check that the

Guzzi's jewel-like 254. With an engine capacity of 231.1cc, each cylinder was a mere 57.825cc.

254 which you are thinking of buying has a *metal* tank. Many of the early versions had a plastic one (which is illegal in certain countries). Don't be fooled by the outer cover, the real tank is a separate container (holding 8.5 litres) hidden away under all the plastic exterior. Generally the finish is much higher than the larger fours (there is a lot less chromework!). Engine life depends on regular oil/filter changes, so you have been warned... Provided these are carried out it is a reliable little unit, but laziness in this area can easily spell disaster. Parts can be expensive, if you can find them.

### Star rating: four firm stars
By far the most collectable of the bikes featured in this chapter. I predict that prices will go much higher. This really is one for the collectors, even though it was not a sales success for the company.

### 125 2C 4T
Besides the 250 TS two-stroke, there was another Guzzi parallel twin. This machine, a four-stroke named the 125 2C 4T, was in effect one-half of the 254. This had an actual capacity of 123.57cc, using the 254's original stroke of 38mm, but with the bore increased to 45.5mm. With a single overhead camshaft driven by a chain between the two barrels, and a pair of Dell'Orto PHBG 20B carburettors, the miniature twin pumped out a healthy 16 bhp at 10,600 rpm and a 5-speed gearbox helped to keep the tiny unit on the boil.

The 125 Guzzi made extensive use of the 254's running gear. These included Guzzi/Benelli sealed damper forks, a 260mm Brembo disc at the front, Sebac rear shocks, and many of the electrical components, including push-button starting (and like the four, there was no back-up kickstarter).

Price was once again a problem, which meant that it was only on the protected home market that the small four-stroke twin made any sales progress, and then only in small

Intended mainly for Italian market needs, the 125 2C 4T was manufactured between 1979 and 1983.

The power unit of the 125 4T twin, clearly derived from the quarter-litre four.

numbers. After making its first appearance at Milan in 1979, the 2C 4T went on sale shortly afterwards, remaining available until 1983.

### What to look for
Although it was physically the same size as the 254, it lacked the performance (Guzzi claimed 74 mph), or the glamour, and should be avoided.

### Star rating: one solitary star
Unpopular new, unpopular now.

### Summary
The 254 is the only one in this section really worth finding, as it represents one of the truly great Italian bikes of the late 1970s — even though much of its engineering owes more to Tokyo than Mandello del Lario. It was the first 4-cylinder quarter-litre to make it to series production and this assures its place in motorcycling history. The other Guzzi fours are far less notable, whilst the 125 twin is hardly worth a mention.

# CHAPTER 13

# Heavyweight Cruisers

| | | |
|---|---|---|
| ** | V1000 Convert | 1975-84 |
| *** | 1000 G5 | 1978-83 |
| ** | T3 California | 1975-80 |
| *** | California II | 1981-87 |
| * | 1000 SP (Spada) | 1978-80 |
| *** | 1000 SP NT | 1980-83 |
| * | 1000 SP II (16 in F/W) | 1984-86 |
| *** | 1000 SP II (18in F/W) | 1986-88 |

Special note: In the USA, G5s and Converts are worth next to nothing, SPs and Californias sell for almost twice as much (especially the California)

## History

Ever since the first V7 appeared during the mid-1960s there has been at least one large-capacity Guzzi V-twin offered in touring guise. The big vees make excellent long-distance bikes. The concept brings together an excellent blend of reliability, simplicity, performance and economy.

## V1000 Convert

The V1000 Convert was a revolutionary motorcycle, but one which ultimately proved a sales failure. Starting with the 1975 model line Guzzi offered its customers an automatic (that is semi-automatic) model. The idea was to release the rider from the need to operate the clutch lever and gear lever, which together with the linked braking system meant that three of the main controls were made redundant. However, Guzzi chose to leave all three of these controls on the machine. But their role was merely supplementary, for only the throttle and foot brake were needed to put the V1000 through the most demanding series of manoeuvres. Operating only the throttle, the standing ¼-mile could be achieved in 15.2 seconds, together with a terminal speed of 88 mph, just one second and two miles per hour slower than a standard 5-speed 850 Guzzi.

Once again the development of the V1000 came, as with the V7, from the company's involvement with police work. In fact as long ago as 1972 a modified 850 GT had been tested by the Los Angeles Police Department. When the production version (by now mounted in an 850 T3 chassis) was released three years later it required a confirmed Guzzi buff to 'double take' to spot the shiftless bike. In fact the outer modifications were extremely limited.

A clutch, but of different design, was retained. There was a hydraulic torque converter, backed up by a two-speed reduction gear, which took the place of the conventional 5-speed gearset. Explained simply, a torque converter is two facing multi-blade vanes or fans in a sealed drum of fluid. The engine-powered front vane moves the fluid, which in turn applies hydraulic pressure to the rear output vane, thus motivating it to turn in unison. The two-speed gearbox provides high and low ranges for optional use, with engagement made through a mechanical lever and conventional clutch. Low range, for example, can be engaged for extended heavy traffic or mountainous work; engagement can be made on the move with a flick of the clutch. Low range, naturally, provides more

The large-capacity Guzzi V-twin touring models, like this 1975 V1000 Convert, can corner with the best of them.

responsive acceleration and is good up to 80 mph. But for the open road the high range would normally be used.

What does it feel like? The engine revs come up considerably quicker than a conventional gearbox upon moving off the mark, but this quickly levels off as momentum builds to what is to be full lock-up once the machine is up to its cruising speed range.

Noticeable at first, the rider soon becomes accustomed to the different sensations of sound and movement. An average getaway requires more throttle than normal, and until such time as the new rider (to the V1000) becomes acquainted with the characteristic he is apt to think he is almost riding a large-capacity moped. But once acclimatized, however, the V1000 feels smoother than the manual models, since it is not accompanied

by the usual slight wriggle and lurch of the torque reaction from the final drive occasioned by engine speed during the gearchange.

The torque converter (made by the German Sachs company) is sandwiched between the clutch and two-speed gearbox. Two hydraulic pipes are visible from the outside. Fluid is stored in a tank underneath the seat and circulated by means of a pump on the end of the camshaft.

Acceleration is deceptive, since the engine never peaks but rather seems to be holding a relatively constant speed. There is virtually no engine braking (almost like a two-stroke) and so the brakes are used more than on the conventional Guzzi V-twins.

The question of power loss-efficiency through the torque converter was anticipated by the use, for the first time on a Guzzi, of

V1000 engine unit. Note the torque converter fluid pipes (just below the carburettor). Otherwise, externally, it is difficult to tell automatic and manual engines apart.

the 1000cc class engine size. The exact capacity is 948.813cc (88×78mm). These engine dimensions were subsequently employed by Guzzi on models such as the G5, SP and Le Mans IV.

The frame was the factory's well-proven and good-handling full duplex loop with split bottom rails, first seen on the V7 Sport and later on most of the other models, including the 850T/T3 series and Le Mans. Most of the cycle parts were shared with the T3, including the front and rear suspension, and spoked, alloy rim Borrani wheels. The stainless steel mudguards were identical, as were the painted steel side panels, except for their 'V1000' badges. The fuel tank was outwardly the same, but incorporated a fuel gauge which was fitted into the offside front of the tank and activated a warning light on the instrument console.

The latter was new to the V1000. Mounted on the clamps of the standard-issue T3-type high handlebars, it was a massive, square-section black plastic casing moulded in two sections. The centre of the console was dominated by an equally large Veglia speedometer (with a face diameter of around 150mm) and no tachometer was fitted. On either side were a mass of warning lights, five per side and a pair of flick switches, together with a trip button for resetting the speedo odometer.

The handlebar controls were also standard T3 components, but on early V1000s a triangular master cylinder was fitted to the brake lever operating the right-hand front disc. On post-1976 models this was replaced by a conventional Brembo round master cylinder used on the other vees.

The multiplicity of warning lights on the

A V1000 polished to perfection on the company's stand at the Milan Show, November 1975. Although it remained on Guzzi's list for some eight years, sales were never more than a trickle.

The manual version of the V1000, the G5. Basically the same bike, except for conventional 5-speed box and the addition of a tachometer.

V1000's instrument console reflected a particular interest in 'safety' features on this bike. To warn of low brake fluid level, the rear brake master cylinder cap incorporated a switch, and another switch linked to the side-stand prevented the engine being started until the stand was retracted. When in use, the side-stand also activated a mechanical brake caliper, enabling the rider to park his machine on a hill. This system was cable operated and worked on the rear disc brake.

Three colour schemes were offered, black, silver and metallic ice blue. Black could be specified with a choice of either gold or white striping and the other two colours had black lining.

One of the most outstanding features of the bike was its seat, the most comfortable I have ever experienced on an Italian machine.

The specifications was completed by a number of accessories as standard equipment, including an hydraulic steering damper, panniers, front and rear crashbars, tinted screen, heel-and-toe 'gearchange' lever (for selecting high or low ratio), a larger rear light with plastic cover and small aerofoils mounted on the front crashbars. Models built after 1979 featured cast alloy wheels.

Although it remained in production for almost a decade the V1000, like the Honda 400 and 750 automatics, never quite made it. Unlike their four-wheeled cousins, motorcyclists just have not accepted the 'auto' option.

## 1000 G5

Essentially a manual version of the V1000, the G5 was offered between 1979 and 1983. The other differences included cast alloy wheels and a small rev counter. Performance was also improved (by around 10 per cent). This combined with the easier state of the spares position makes it a better buy than the 'auto'.

## T3 California

When importers Coburn and Hughes relaunched the Guzzi range to British riders in the spring of 1975, the 850 T3 was priced at £1599 and the T3 California at £1699. The

extra £100 gave you an American-inspired custom package comprising a toughened tinted perspex screen, a set of braced 'high-and-wide' laid-back western bars, an hydraulic steering damper, knee protectors on the cylinder head, a large black and white 'buddy' seat with chrome grab rail, lockable glass-fibre panniers on chrome plated frames, and a carrier and front and rear crashbars in the same finish. The California treatment was completed by a pair of rider's footboards, a set of revised controls which included a heel-and-toe gear lever and a much larger (and superior in operation) side-stand, which could be operated by the rider from the saddle.

In all other aspects the 'Cali' as it soon became universally called, was the same as its T3 brother. So for all other information refer to the 850 T3 section in Chapter 10.

From the 1979 model year the California was 'updated' with a locking petrol filler cap, plastic alternator cover, CEV headlamp and SP switchgear.

## California II

The next development was a brand new California, the II, which was launched at the Milan Show in November 1981. This was a rather strange mixture of both old and new, with a return to styling not dissimilar to the original V850 GT California (see Chapter 9), while its engine was updated by employing the square 'slab'-style cylinder heads and barrels first used on the Le Mans III.

Like the Le Mans III, the new California was substantially different from the bike it replaced. Not only was its detail specification and appearance altered, but its engine capacity was upped to 948cc. This was achieved in the same way as with the V1000 and G5, by increasing the bore size to 88mm.

Although Guzzi *claimed* almost 120 mph, reality was somewhat different, and with the various accessories such as screen, panniers and crashbars in place the California II was only just able to creep past 105 mph. Not only this, but at around 90 mph, or sometimes a shade less, depending on conditions, an unsettling weave would set in. This can also prove a problem with other Guzzi V-twins using the large upright tinted

The 850 T3 California was virtually a standard T3 with customizing equipment. The package included tinted screen, panniers, front and rear crash-bars, large (but uncomfortable!) buddy seat and footboards.

windshield, which in my experience simply creates an excess of wind pressure at speeds above 80 mph.

Besides the obvious differences in the style of components such as panniers, mudguards and the like, together with the 'square' top end of the engine, there were other changes. One of these centred around the increase in the length of the swinging arm to 470mm between centres, and additional bracing over earlier models.

The California II also benefitted from new machine tools which had been fitted at the factory. These allowed closer working tolerances to be employed. Along with the fitment of aluminium rocker supports, this produced a much quieter engine, whilst the addition of the improved air filtration system

pioneered on the Le Mans III, plus a less noisy exhaust system, ensured that the larger California was more civilized than before.

As proof that Guzzi had hit the right formula the California II proved an excellent seller both in Italy and abroad during the early 1980s, having created a niche market position all to itself – between the ultra expensive and heavyweight Harley-Davidson Electra Glide and the cheaper but generally unloved Japanese custom bikes.

The California III arrived in 1988 and continues the theme today. Two versions are available. One is a cruiser with a clear windscreen, the other has a full fairing and panniers.

The California version of T3 cost £100 more than the basic model when it went on sale in the UK during May 1975.

The California II was noticeably different from the original. It went on sale in early 1982, after making its début at Milan in late 1981.

The control layout of California II.

## 1000 SP

It there was ever any suspicion that Moto Guzzi were deliberately trying harder each year to steal market share from BMW in the shaft-drive stakes, then the 1978 1000 SP would leave absolutely no doubt. The SP (Spada in Britain) obviously owed an awful lot to the success of the BMW R100 RS – one look at the fairing tells all.

In essence the SP's engine was the same as the V1000, but with a conventional Guzzi car-type clutch and 5-speed gearbox. And except for the unswept silencers, cast alloy wheels, less well-padded upholstery and minor details such as different rear brake pads and a sensor valve which automatically reduced the hydraulic pressure should either wheel start to lock under excessively heavy braking it was very much like the 850 T3, except of course for the fairing.

Several ideas were tested in Guzzi's own wind tunnel before the final selection was made. And generally the basic shape was right, because it has lasted 13 years without any major alteration. By the standards prevailing at the time, Guzzi's solution was elegant and somewhat unconventional. Even though the streamlining provided the rider with the protection of a full fairing, the design was closer to the traditional combination of a separate handlebar fairing and legshields. The logic was good, as the top section could turn with the handlebars, allowing it to be mounted much closer to the rider than a conventional full fairing, which needs to be far enough away to allow clearance for the handlebars on full lock. There was also the bonus in that the lower side panels, which were securely mounted to the frame, could be removed individually

Early SP1000 models suffered from awful finish and
poor seating . . .

. . .SPNT (new type) does not look much different,
but was a vastly superior bike. The paint and
chromework were more durable, the seat from

V1000 supremely comfortable. Other minor
improvements were also introduced.

The wind tunnel-tested fairing was both efficient
and practical.

without disturbing the main top section — a definite plus for maintenance purposes.

Running on a compression ratio of 9.2:1 the 1000 SP offered a combination of a 120 mph maximum speed, excellent rider protection and outstanding fuel economy — at a cheaper price than BMW.

These were therefore the attributes of the original SP, but there were snags, unfortunately, for Guzzi and its customers (most of all its customers). This apparently ideal concept was ruined by a combination of spartan comfort and abysmal finish. The best fairing offered up to that time was ruined by the awful finish and often lopsided fitment, poor design of the louvres which crushed kneecaps with relish for tall riders, and the 'Heath Robinson' fitting brackets, which enabled one to flake off what little paint there was with each screw removed. The seat on the SP 'Mark I' was painfully uncomfortable (especially for the pillion passenger) after anything over an hour in the saddle, whilst the general paintwork and chrome plating were almost wafer thin. A choice of awkward to match metallic gold or silver paint did not help matters either.

## 1000 SP NT

Eventually the spate of disgruntled owners' moans and groans reached the Guzzi management back at Mandello del Lario. The result was the SP NT, launched in early 1980. In truth the NT (new type) was hardly a new model, just how the original bike should have been in the first place. At first glance, except for the fresh livery in either pale metallic green or metallic ice blue, and new 'flat' low-line silencers, nothing appeared to be different between the Mark I and the NT. It is not until one gets aboard the NT that one notices all the changes.

Gone were the knee-crunching louvres, which were replaced by wider, more suitably placed components. The seat was now the same as the deliciously soft V1000 type; whilst the screen appeared to have jumped an inch of so (matching the increase in seat height!). The new-style Lafranconi silencers were fatter and more bulbous and more effective. They also had thicker plating than the originals and lasted longer. The footrests

were now more sanely positioned, providing comfort to both rider and passenger.

Other differences included chromed rear shock absorber springs and silver fork sliders (formerly black), whilst the rocker box covers had been polished on the flat top section. A flat lockable cover hid the filling orifice on the fuel tank and the exhaust header pipes were now double skinned to withstand the usual instant 'blueing' achieved by the Mark I. The frame, originally the truly vile 'peel off' matt black as on the early Le Mans, was now gloss-painted, albeit still rather thinly in places.

Technically, except for Nicasil cylinder bores, these was nothing really new, just that the NT was a complete package, the original Mark I was not.

## 1000 SP II (16 in F/W)

In November 1983, the Milan Show was again the setting for the appearance of a new SP. Coded SP II, it was substantially altered in many important aspects. Its power plant now featured the angular cylinder head and barrel finning seen on the Le Mans III, California II and 850 T5 models. The revised cylinder heads brought maximum power up to 67 bhp at 6700 rpm — although effective torque figures were slightly reduced. But it was to the running gear that the major changes had occurred.

The bike's appearance was noticeably changed. Major amongst the changes was the fitment of a 16 in front wheel; whilst both cast wheels now sported ten straight spokes rather than the original 12 cranked ones. Wider section tyres, a 100/90 H16 front and 130/80 H18 rear, provided increased levels of road grip. The brake disc diameter had now been standardized to 270mm all round, and these were drilled and plated, which provided them with a different style.

The basic chassis remained as it had when the original SP was launched, but it was now dressed in a virtually new set of clothes. One component which had not been altered was the fairing. But behind it was a totally new tank shape with an increased 26-litre capacity. Also new were the seat and passenger grab rail, the mudguards (now in plastic) and the side panels. One small

Rider's-eye view of SP1000 NT.

change which broke with Guzzi tradition was that twin windtone horns replaced the previous type that had been a feature of Guzzi V-twins for almost two decades.

The finish was in red and black throughout, with red employed on the tank, side panels and fairing. Black was used for the frame, lower forks, cylinder recesses in the fairing and the rocker covers.

Although the appearance was attractive, and the performance, weather protection and economy impressive, the effect was totally ruined by the truly awful handling and road holding thanks to that 16 in front wheel. How could Guzzi have made such a monumental error? As explained elsewhere it was the unfortunate result of development being undertaken by a combination of four-wheel engineers and marketing men rather than motorcyclists.

The SP II featured many changes to both the engine and running gear, some not always for the best. Many did not like the Le Mans III-type square finning for the heads and barrels (even though the technical improvements were worthwhile).

The SP1000 II tested by the author in 1985 for *Motorcycle Enthusiast*. The handling was marred by the use of a 16in front wheel, in much the same way as the 850 T5 and early Le Mans 1000 (Mk IV).

## 1000 SP II (18 in F/W)

It took Guzzi a little under two years to learn the lesson. Common sense prevailed and the SP, together with the Le Mans, were given back their 18 in front wheels. At a stroke this solved the bend swinging problems and buyers returned. The balance of the technical specification remained unchanged. In this guise the 1000 SP soldiered on until it was superseded by the considerably updated 'III' version for the 1988 season. This is described in Chaper 15 – *Latest Developments*, and comes with, or without fuel injection. The Mille GT was introduced in 1989. Although it's a touring bike, it is essentially a Le Mans without the fairing or bodywork. Again see Chapter 15 for its full specification.

## What to look for

V1000: parts problems. Replacement of torque converter assembly likely to be horrendously expensive. Lack of braking from engine. Restricted performance. Ensure all switches are in working order.

1000 G5: less exotic, but far more practical than the auto version.

T3 California: essentially a dressed up T3. Seat uncomfortable. Handling over 80 mph (with screen) weird.

California II: More of a purpose-built custom cruiser than the T3 inspired 'Cali'. Improved seat. Performance still restricted by upright screen.

1000 SP: good idea as a competitor to BMW's R100 RS, but poor seat and abysmal finish let it down.

1000 SP NT: much improved in all departments together with a comfy seat and better finish (but still not as good as BMW).

1000 SP II (16 in F/W): potentially good bike ruined by awful handling from the 16 in front wheel. Go for the later version with an 18 in wheel.

1000 SP II (18 in F/W): safe handling again, finish improving, but still not in the BMW class.

**Star rating: 1000 G5, California II, 1000 SP NT and 1000 SP II (18in F/W) three firm stars: T3 California and V1000 two stars; 1000 SP II (16in F/W) and 1000 SP a single star for less than perfect bikes**

Anyone purchasing a 1000 G5, California II or 1000 SPNT/SP II (18in F/W) should not be disappointed *provided* that they take their time in selecting a well-looked-after example. All are excellent bikes and generally a pleasure to own and ride. Conversely they are never likely to be considered collectable, hence the middle-of-the-road ratings.

The T3 California is a 'tarty' dressed-to-kill version of the standard T3, and not half as practical to live with every day – not worth more than two stars.

The V1000 also only gains two stars – but this is mainly associated with potential parts problems rather than ability.

As for the 1000 SP II (16in F/W) or 1000 SP my advice is *do not bother*. They both suffer glaring faults which should never have been present in the first place. Their solitary star rating reflects these failings, and they are best ignored by potential buyers, unless they are extremely cheap.

# CHAPTER 14

# Smaller Vees

| | | |
|---|---|---|
| ** | V35 | 1977-79 |
| ** | V50 | 1977-79 |
| ** | V50 II | 1979-80 |
| *** | V50 III | 1981-85 |
| *** | V50 Monza | 1980-83 |
| *** | V35 Imola | 1979-83 |
| * | V35/50/65 Custom | 1982-85 |
| *** | V35 II | 1980-85 |
| *** | V65 & V65 SP | 1982-85 |
| *** | V35/V65 TT | 1984-86 |
| *** | V35 Imola II, V50 Monza II | |
| * | V65 Lario | 1984-87 |
| * | V35 III | 1985-87 |
| * | V75 | 1985-87 |

Special note: In the USA Monzas are quite rare and sought after. They are still not expensive, but they sell immediately when offered.

## History

Guzzi boss Alejandro De Tomaso wanted to double the factory's production from its 1975 figures by the end of 1978. To do this the Argentinian-born industrialist realized that it would need a new range of middleweight machines based around the marque's excellent reputation for its larger V-twins, so De Tomaso instructed chief designer Lino Tonti to come up with a suitable machine. Technically the result was everything that De Tomaso could have wished, and was based around the 90-degree V-twin ohv four-stroke with shaft drive layout that had proved so successful with the larger machines.

Emerging initially as the V35 and V50, Guzzi's new middleweight made its public bow at the West German Cologne Show in September 1976. Later the larger V65 and V75 were added, together with a host of derivatives in standard, sports, custom and trial guises, making it the factory's most important and influential design of the late 1970s and early 1980s.

Small numbers of both the V35 and V50 were manufactured in 1977 and 1978, but it was not until production got under way at the former Innocenti plant in Milan during late 1978 that the real story began. This was because, quite simply, Guzzi's Mandello del Lario base was already fully stretched during this period producing the larger V-twin models.

The world's press (and distributors) had already tested early examples of the new design and it had generally received rave reviews. To this could be added two other important features which made the Guzzi middleweights such strong contenders: price and an incredibly low weight – a mere 350 lb (152kg) dry. These factors combined to make the V50 both lighter *and* cheaper than Honda's best-selling CX500 in Britain during 1979.

## V35/V50

The engine units of the V35 and V50 shared identical external dimensions, but a bore and stroke of 66×50.6mm for the V35 and 74×57mm for the V50 gave them capacities of 346.23cc and 490.30cc respectively. The V35's maximum crankshaft power rating was 33.6 bhp at 8100 rpm, while the larger unit produced 45 bhp at 7500 rpm. To take account of this, the primary drive ratios were different, with 1.846 on the 350 and 1.642 on the 500, and the helical gears in the final drive were also matched to the output, with 13/24 and 14/23 respectively.

Both engines ran on compression ratios of 10.8:1, and like the larger V-twins, the piston and cylinder barrel were matched in either A, B or C codings. The cylinder bores were Nicasil coated.

The pistons were of the three-ring type, and they were unusual in featuring concave crowns. This resulted from the cylinder head design, which did not follow traditional Guzzi practice. Instead of the conventional hemispherical combustion chamber and angled valves, the inside of the head was flat, with both valves parallel. Space for combustion was thus provided in the top of the piston rather than in the head. Although new to Guzzi, the system was well tested, for Heron heads, as they were called, have been applied on Jaguar cars and Morini V-twins, amongst others. Although the exhaust valve head diameters of the V35 and V50 were the same at 27.6mm, the inlets were different: V35: 30.6mm; V50: 32.6mm. Twin coil springs were fitted to each valve, which ran on an iron guide retained in the head by a circlip. Although the inlet valve sizes were different, both machines had identical carburettors, 24mm square slide Dell'Orto VHBZs. A distinctive feature of the new engine was the square finning of both the cylinder heads and barrels. There were also anti-resonance rubber blocks, similar to

A V50 II on display at Mick Walker Motorcycles in late 1979. With a low price and rave press reviews the UK importers sold over 2000 examples that year. But sales fell back after a flood of warranty claims.

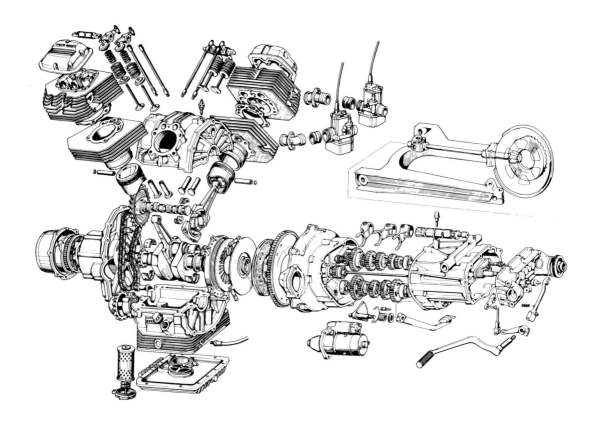

The V50 (and V35) followed the layout of bigger Mandello vees. This exploded view shows the details.

those fitted to many air-cooled two-strokes, to reduce fin ringing.

The crankcase, unlike the larger V-twins, was in two sections, split horizontally and held together by ten studs of varying length. The one-piece crankshaft carried a pair of bolt-up steel con-rods with 15mm gudgeon pins running in bronze small-end bushes. Again, there were Class A (blue) and B (white) con-rods which had been factory matched to crankshafts of the same coding.

The engine was lubricated in a similar way to the larger V-twins, with a lobe-type pump circulating oil at a pressure of between 4.2 and 4.8kg/cm$^2$. However, a new feature was a different design of disposable oil filter housed in the sump. And unlike the bigger

twins, it was possible for this to be replaced with the sump in place.

Transmission was similar to that found in the larger vees, but there were some important variations. As on the bigger bikes, the clutch was housed inside the large-diameter ring gear for the electric starter. But unlike them, the clutch itself was a true single-plate diaphragm type, consisting of a friction plate, pressure cap, pressure plate and diaphragm spring.

The 5-speed constant-mesh gearbox featured frontal engagement, with a left-hand foot lever, and the internal ratios were identical to both the V35 and V50. In addition the gears themselves were straight-cut, rather than helical as on the bigger vees.

Final drive was by the familiar Guzzi shaft, but the universal joint carried a long extension, as on the V1000 model, and was protected by a new design of rubber bellows.

Electrical equipment consisted of a 12-volt 20-amp/hour battery, a Bosch G1(R)14V 20 A21 alternator, and a DG starter motor rated at 0.7 hp from the same source. Bosch also provided the regulator and rectifier, as well as the electronic ignition system (which was made up of a pair of magnetic pick-up units and two transducers). Completing the electrics were a 170mm CEV headlight, a twin-bulb rear light, black indicator bodies, single Belli horn and a cluster of four warning lights on the instrument console. The handlebar switchgear was the same garish 'Monopoly' type found on some of the larger models.

The frame design followed the larger vees by having detachable bottom tubes which allowed the engine to be removed from below with ease. In fact, the whole drive system, engine, gearbox, drive shaft and rear wheel, together with the exhaust system, can be detached from the frame, forks and front wheel to provide almost unmatched accessibility.

The swinging arm was a one-piece cast alloy affair, pivoting on the rear of the gearbox casting, suspended from the tubular frame by three or five way adjustable Sebac rear shocks. Front forks were of Guzzi's own design and of 35mm-stanchion diameter. As on the larger models these featured sealed internal damper units. Steering head bearings consisted of cups, cones and ball bearings.

Wheels were cast alloy with 12 spokes and painted silver. Braking was triple cast-iron discs (twin 260mm at the front and a single 235mm at the rear) with Brembo calipers. There was the familiar patented linked system, but what was different was the front brake reservoir, which was tucked out of harm's way at the front of the petrol tank and connected to the lever by a short length of Bowden brake cable.

Both models shared the same colour choice, either bright red or metallic blue/grey. These main colours were used on the tank, side panels, mudguards and headlamp brackets, while the frame, headlamp shell and many smaller items were finished in black. Like the wheels, the fork sliders (bottom outers) and swinging arm were painted silver and the entire exhaust system was chrome plated. As well as the body colour, the tank was also equipped with a hinged panel (in black) which hid the fuel filler cap and a front brake master cylinder.

None of the V35 and V50s from the 1977 or 1978 production batches was imported into Britain.

## V50 II

It was only with the introduction of the V50 II in early 1979 that exports of the new Guzzi middleweight began (the V35 was mainly for the home market). There were also a number of changes, mainly of a cosmetic nature.

The oil capacity was upped from 2.25 to 2.50 litres by making the finned sump casting deeper, with a different gasket. In place of the circular alloy timing cover came a black plastic moulding (presumably for cost reasons). There were also a few smaller differences such as polished rocker covers in place of the original matt finish.

The black CEV indicators were replaced by chrome Larghi components, a matching chrome finish was applied to the indicator support brackets and the headlamp rim. The bottom yoke was now polished rather than black.

The paintwork was more elaborate (although of no better quality) with thin lining in orange and yellow running on either side of the tank and on the side panels above and below the badges. These latter items now incorporated 'II' in addition to V50.

There were also a number of changes made for specific export markets. These included: USA, where the V50 had side reflectors fitted to the indicators, a sealed beam headlamp and other minor modifications to meet existing American legislation. The Dutch market V50 had modified exhaust pipes; whilst the Germans received a batch of V35s with smaller carburettors and valves.

The British importers, Coburn and Hughes, simply imported Italian specification bikes (V50s only – no V35s at

The V50 III introduced improvements to both mechanics and finish. The paint stayed on longer and a return to points in place of electronic ignition cured an annoying mid-range flat spot.

this time) with mph speedometers. These bikes did not even have a headlamp that dipped on the correct side, much to the annoyance of many customers. UK imports began in April 1979 and by the end of that year over 2000 had been sold, the best opening performance ever by an Italian bike in the British marketplace.

This was largely achieved thanks to the low price, some excellent press reports and the fact that, at least on paper, the V50 II was an impressive bike. The mood of the day is best portrayed by these extracts from *Motorcycle Sport* dated July 1979: 'First impressions of the Guzzi on taking it out for a ride are favourable... The gearchange quality is really good and it's easy to forget that this is a shaft drive machine... Handling is light, accurate and reminiscent of the Ducati single... For going fast it it not a bad idea to ride a machine capable of stopping in good time as well. On this score the Guzzi must achieve 10 out of 10 from anyone... The very high standard of finish, which seems superior to other Guzzis, may be in part due to the new factory... Its most noticeable feature is an 'engine' rather than a 'motor' and one that pulls very well... I predict that the V50 will be an immense success with the UK market.'

All fine words indeed, but unfortunately behind the scenes many of the dealers (and their customers) were none too happy, for the V50 was generating not only a large number of sales, but a depressingly large number of warranty claims.

The most common of these ailments centred around the poor finish; most notably the truly awful paintwork, which was not helped by a rust-trap of a steel front mudguard, shiny plastic side panels which had also been painted (why not leave them colour impregnated), with the result that the paint simply 'fell off', and as if this was not bad enough, chromework which was not much better, thanks to items such as rot-prone silencers.

Technical problems were also present, including tricky electrics – particularly the ignition switch. There were also oil seal failures in the final drive shaft-flange and front forks, plus a suspension system which seemed to sag within a relatively short time. All these problems meant that after a few months sales dropped off alarmingly.

## V50 III

So in mid-1980 the Mark III appeared. Generally it had a much superior finish, a plastic front mudguard instead of the V50 II's rust-prone metal item, a halogen headlamp, black indicators (now oblong) and stems, while the brake calipers were moved from in front of the fork legs to behind.

There were mechanical changes as well. Both valve sizes were increased, as was the carburettor choke diameter, and the exhaust and inlet plumbing was less restrictive (Guzzi claimed it resulted in an extra 2 bhp). But the major changes lay under that black plastic circular cover at the front of the crankcases. The Mark II's electronic ignition disappeared to be replaced by old-fashioned twin contract breakers and twin condensers, whilst the simplex cam chain was uprated to a duplex affair, with a spring-loaded tensioner.

The ignition re-think killed two birds with one stone. It eliminates an annoying flat spot midway through the rev-range and it was less expensive for the factory in component parts. Other changes from the 'II' to the 'III' were a new front indicator mounting incorporating a grille and Moto Guzzi emblem; revised headlamp brackets, colour-coded rear light support, a new dual-seat and redesigned instrument console.

The front brake master cylinder was relocated from under the hinged lid on the tank to the more normal handlebar location adjacent to the brake lever, which now operated it directly. The brake discs themselves were now drilled. The area formerly occupied by the master cylinder reservoir was taken up by a modified cover for the fuel filler cap. There was now a chrome fuel filler cap.

Colour choices had become red or brown, and the matt black upper panel on the tank was dispensed with, while the rear light was finished integrally with the plastic mudguard. Finally the side panel now read 'V50 III'. Sales picked up again, but never quite reached those heady days of 1979.

## V35 Imola and V50 Monza

The first of these, the V35 Imola, made its début at the 1979 Milan Show. In appearance the Imola looked a real darling, but looks can sometimes deceive. Except for larger valves (30.5mm inlet, 27.5mm exhaust), the Imola had exactly the same engine specification as the V35 II. Press reports of the era gave a wide range of output figures up to a high of 36 bhp. The true figure was 27.83 bhp at the rear wheel. This gave a maximum speed of 94 mph sitting upright and 99 mph with the rider well tucked in behind the mini-fairing and chin buried into the tank.

The majority of the running gear was shared with the V35 II, but the little sportster gained a small fairing (similar to that fitted to the Benelli 900 Sei), clip-ons, rearsets, a new dualseat with a racing-style tailpiece, unswept silencers and indicators from the V50 III.

Roadholding and handling qualities were improved even further by air-assisted suspension front and rear, the latter units now being exclusively of Paoli manufacture. A larger 16-litre fuel tank was fitted together with new side panels and other more minor components. There were no badges or lining, only a gold 'Moto Guzzi' eagle transfer on the front of the fairing and each side of the tank, and V35 Imola logos on the side panels.

The V35 Imola was really intended as a tax breaker special for the Italian and French markets. There was also a V40 Imola for Japanese enthusiasts. But most export customers wanted a 500 version, and Guzzi gave it to them with the V50 Monza displayed at the Bologna Show in 1980. This featured a standard V50 III engine, but with a taller ratio in the rear hub, so a Monza would do 70 mph in top with 1000 rpm less on the

The V35 II engine; built mainly to take advantage of Italian tax laws, the V35 none the less had a character all its own. The engine was smooth, quiet and economical, but lacked any real power.

An attractive little sportster. The V35 Imola (together with the similar larger capacity V50 Monza) offered riders a more sporting stance. The performance, however, was little different from 'cooking' models.

tachometer than a standard Mark III. Colours were either red or metallic blue/grey. When *Motorcycling* magazine tested a Monza in 1980 they recorded an electronically timed 105.35 mph and a fuel consumption figure of 58 mpg overall.

## V35 II

In line with improvements to the V50, the V35 had also been updated (but only once) when a new version, the V35 II, made its bow at the Milan Show in November 1979. Put simply, it was the V50 II chassis whilst the engine now sported larger inlet manifolds and carburettors (26mm) and new silencers of the V50 III type. Essentially it was a better bike than the original, in the same way that the V50 III was superior to the earlier marks.

## V65

To many the V65 was everything the V50 should have been. The 500 (and even more so the 350) just could not compete with the 4-cylinder opposition coming from the Land of the Rising Sun. But common sense stretched beyond peak power figures into the realms of peak running costs. The 500 *should* have been the bike to realize Guzzi's potential: easy to get on with, a true everyday machine. It did not fully make it because it lacked the power. In an era when 250s were nudging the 100 mph mark, the V50 scuttled across the line a bare 3 to 4 mph quicker; more to the point, even in Mark III form, it lacked real mid-range power.

Many enthusiasts were soon asking for a 650 version, but this was a long time coming (at least for several export markets, including Britain), with supplies not arriving until 1983 (two years earlier in Italy). Its 643cc (80×64mm) engine gave 52 bhp (at the crankshaft), which provided enough steam to propel the 165kg (363 lb) machine to 111 mph (*Motor Cycle Mechanics*, October 1984 test figures). Even more important was the improved mid-range torque and superior throttle response. There was also an SP with a Spada-type three-piece fairing.

This frontal view of 1980 V50 Monza shows off the
narrow angle of the V-twin engine to good effect.

The V50 Monza controls, instruments, switchgear and inner fairing details.

### V35, V50 and V65 Custom

Although 'Custom' bikes these three models used a large number of stock Guzzi parts; the kicked-up silencers from the Imola/Monza and chrome headlamp brackets from the 850 T3, for example. There is not much point in expensive tooling-up for a concept which at best has only limited fashion appeal, so all three C models were basically standard bikes given a peanut tank (albeit with a useful 15-litre (3.42-gallon) capacity), chrome mudguards, stepped seat, high handlebars and 16in rear wheel.

None sold very well in the export arena, although in the early 1980s they were popular in Italy. The customizing process robbed the machines of some of the best features encountered on the standard versions as the following extract from the July 1986 test of a V35 Custom in *Motorcycle Enthusiast* shows: 'I'd just start to enjoy riding the bike when I'd have to brake or want to change line suddenly, and I'd be back

to indifference again. I feel the use of high bars and small back wheel have marred what is, in standard trim, a good handling machine and, for the price, there are just as simple, yet less agricultural machines on the market'. A saving grace, at least for 'shorties' was the very low seat height, which proved popular with female riders.

### V35/65 TT

The TT did not stand for the Isle of Man TT; instead it meant *Tutto Terreno* (all-terrain). From an industry more famous for its rip-snorting, fire-breathing two-stroke enduro bikes, this Guzzi on/off road offering was the height of civility. Like the Custom models, there was no change in engine specification from the standard V35/V65 models, but cosmetically the pair of TTs were strikingly different from the usual crop of trail bikes. Topped off by a motocross-style 14-litre tank, the layout was extremely effective with smooth, flowing lines that continued through the side panels, and rear seat/mudguard section. The seat covering was in a fashionable red with 'TT' emblazoned in blue and a nose at the front which extended up and over the rear of the tank. The switchgear remained unchanged, as did the matching tacho and speedo. Only a prop-stand was fitted, but a couple of useful additions were rubber gaiters for the special leading-axle Marzocchi 35mm forks and a large rubber mudflap which extended down to protect the timing cover at the base of the front mudguard.

At the front, the enduro-style square headlamp had a plastic cowling with a red number plate at the top and a series of air grilles below. This supported the front direction indicators, which were in black plastic and flexibly mounted on rubber stalks. The tail section, which doubled as part of the rear mudguard, also helped to support the rear light, indicators and a rear carrier. A nylon unbreakable motocross front mudguard was colour-coded to the tank, side panels, tail section and front cowl in either white or steel grey. The rest of the machine was in bright red. The exhaust system, finished in black, consisted of a pair of exhaust pipes, a truly massive collector box and a single pipe which then joined up with a silencer mounted high up on the offside of the machine.

Other features included Akront alloy rims, 3.00×21in front and 4.00×18in rear knobbly tyres, front and rear brakes relying on a single Brembo caliper and 260mm drilled discs of conventional operation on both wheels – not linked as on other Guzzi V-twins.

The TTs were a shade too heavy for serious off-road usage, but made great street bikes.

There is however one particular word of warning. Because of the increased angle of the rear drive housing caused by taller

Generally acknowledged as the best of the middleweight Guzzi V-twins, the V65 is here in SP form. It made amends for the V50's lack of power and was reliable in service. Available in Italy from mid-1981, supplies did not reach Britain until 1983.

suspension, the bearing at the front of the housing will starve for oil unless the oil level is topped up *with the rear end raised to compensate.*

**V35 Imola II, V50 Monza II and V65 Lario**

Launched at the same Milan Show in November 1983 as the TT models were a series of new sports models in 350, 500 and 650 engine sizes. Technically what set these apart from earlier Guzzi V-twins was their 4-valve cylinder heads. And, unlike their two-valve brothers of the same capacities they employed angled, not parallel valve layout.

The three bikes were clearly aimed at the sporting enthusiast, and shared a common styling package. This included a sculptured 18-litre tank, side panels and tail section which blended in to provide a similar result to that achieved on the TTs. Many of the lessons learned on the 850 Le Mans III

styling were applied, displayed best by the way the small cockpit fairing and separate aerofoils were designed to deflect the air stream away from the rider, under the fuel tank and over the cylinder heads.

The front mudguard featured a built-in fork brace, for Guzzi had by then learned from other models with plain plastic guards that, without bracing, the fork legs were liable to flex under severe braking – impairing both the handling and roadholding. The forks themselves were still Guzzi's own air-assisted units, but the fork sliders were modified so that the axle was now actually slightly trailing. The gas shocks were of Paoli manufacture. Following contemporary fashion, both wheels were 16 in fitted with 100/90 H16 front and 120/90 H16 rear Pirelli tyres. The brakes used three 270mm drilled discs.

The rider's view was dominated by the thick rubber instrument console, which at its

Guzzi offered the 'C' (Custom) version of the V35 (shown here), the V50 and the V65. Roadholding was sacrificed for style. Popular at home, but not in the UK.

The much underrated V35 TT (and even more so V65 TT). Excellent on/off-road bike which was suprisingly effective in both roles. Its only real failure is over-complex, rust-prone, exhaust system.

Four valves per cylinder was a real disaster for Guzzi – they tried to do it on the cheap and it did not work. The V65 Lario is shown here. Other models included the Imola II, Monza II and V75.

centre sported a massive white-faced Veglia racing tacho, with a smaller speedo and matching voltmeter – à la Le Mans III.

All three four-valvers were finished in the same colours, a choice of red, silver or white. The main colour was applied to the tank, fairing, seat base, fork sliders, mudguards and bellypan.

So how did the four-valve sportsters perform out on the street? Actually performance was somewhat disappointing at the lower end of the rev range with no real improvement over the two-valve models. But mid-range punch was better, and maximum speed improved thanks to better breathing at high rpm. Maximum speed of the V65 Lario I tested for *Motorcycle Enthusiast* was almost 115 mph. Two lasting impressions were of its compact 'Boy Racer' riding position, and how it would 'sit-up' if the brakes were used in a corner, a trait of 16in wheels.

There was a mechanical snag however; when Guzzi carried out the conversion to four valves it had used the standard cams, followers and valves. The conventional camshafts were solid and these proved unable to provide adequate lubrication to the valve gear. The result was a spate of warranty claims, which to the factory's credit were sorted out with a modification kit comprising new hollow camshafts, modified followers (these can be detected by a matt black finish, rather than the original component's polished bright metal) and new valves.

Only the last few months' production had these uprated parts fitted as standard and most had to have the modification kits fitted by the dealer network. By now all should have been changed, but check before buying.

The simply awful V75. Not only was it flawed by the usual troubles with the four-valve-heads, but the fairing was poorly designed and the 16in front wheel destroyed the handling. One to stay clear of.

The cylinder head and carburettor from the V35 Imola II four valves.

## V35 III and V75

Everyone expected the V75 to be a winner. In fact it was just the reverse. This not only suffered the same mechanical fate as the other four-valve models described above, but its combination of 16in front and 18in rear wheels gave vague, most un-Guzzi-type handling and its seat and fairing came in for sharp criticism from the press. *Motor Cycle International* had this to say: 'A potentially nice motor, with four-valve heads, ruined by restrictive carbs and exhaust. The seat is uncomfortable, the styling odd, and the finish shoddy.' And this, except for the fact that it had a more reliable two-valve set-up, was duplicated by the V35 III.

Take my advice and stay well clear of both models.

## What to look for

Besides particular problems already laid out in their respective sections, all of the V35, V50, V65 and V75 series of Guzzi middleweight 90-degree ohv V-twins are prone to burn out valves if a regular check (and adjustment if necessary) is not made to the tappets. I would recommend this to be done at 3000-mile intervals. Another real problem can be neglect. For example, if the front engine mounting belt is not removed regularly and re-greased, it will become seized and an absolute pig to get out. The early models in particular tend to get very scruffy. As a result, the range of secondhand prices varies enormously. My own advice is to pay the extra for a pristine example, which will work out cheaper in the long run.

There were far more V50s sold than other models (at least in Britain) and therefore there are still lots in circulation. Even with all

The V75 had a large moulding which not only housed the instruments, idiot lights and ignition switch, but also hid most of the handlebar from the rider's view. The switch-gear is typical mid-1980s Guzzi issue.

their faults, they seem to go on forever through succeeding disasters and rebuilds in a charming almost agricultural manner – something which few other bikes can achieve.

**Star ratings: Three stars** for most in this category are basically good bikes to own and to ride provided that you accept their shortcomings. *Two stars* early model V35/V50s with several teething problems – better to go for later Marks. *One star* Custom models, V35 III and V75 – my honest advice is stay well clear, particularly of the latter two.

## Summary
The middleweight Guzzi V-twins never quite delivered what they promised. However, those models awarded three stars are the best of the bunch and have provided many riders with affordable Italian biking over the years. None is likely to become a collector's item.

# CHAPTER 15

# Latest Developments

Although the main purpose of the *Illustrated Moto Guzzi Buyer's Guide* is to provide enthusiasts and potential buyers with information on older bikes, the existing Guzzi range are virtually the same type of machines as described in the main text; it has therefore been decided to include the latest (1992) model range.

The models described are of 650, 750 and 1000cc classes. Most are available in Britain and the United States, but some like the NTX and Quota are not, due to their plastic fuel tanks. It should also be noted that several of the 650 and 750cc models have 350 versions for the Italian domestic market. The 1000 Daytona is largely the work of the American, Dr John Wittner.

Prices quoted are those as at December 1991, including British VAT (Valued Added Tax) and Car Tax.

The British distributors are:

**Three Cross (Imports) Ltd**
Woolsbridge Industrial Estate
6 Old Barn Farm Road
Three Legged Cross
Wimborne
Dorset
BH21 6SP

Tel: 0202 824531/2/3

Fax: 0202 823056

In January 1991, Moto Guzzi North America (a subsidiary of Maserati North America) was purchased by Fran Contaldi (Moto Guzzi NA's former marketing director) and renamed Moto America Incorporated.

Moto America is the sole Guzzi importer for both the United States and Canada. Their address is 1004 Main Street, Lillington, North Carolina 27546.

Moto America is importing (Spring 1991) the Mille GT, the SP III, and the 1000 S. It plans to stock the new Daytona model as soon as it is available.

# V65 Florida

| | |
|---|---|
| **Engine:** | 643.6cc 90-degree V-twin ohv. |
| **Bore stoke:** | 80×64mm. |
| **Compression ratio:** | 10:1. |
| **Transmission:** | primary by helical gears, secondary by cardan shaft and bevel gears. |
| **Clutch:** | single disc, dry-type. |
| **Fuel delivery:** | 2 Dell'Orto PHBH 30 carburettors. |
| **Electrical system:** | 12-volt, alternator 14V-20A, rectifier and regulator. 20 amp hour battery. |
| **Starting:** | electric. |
| **Ignition:** | electronic, magnetic pick-up. |
| **Gearbox:** | 5-speed. |

| | |
|---|---|
| **Brakes:** | front, twin 260mm disc; rear, single 235mm disc. |
| **Wheels:** | cast alloy or spoked option 18 in F, 16 in R. |
| **Instrument panel:** | speedometer, tachometer and warning lights. |
| **Fuel tank capacity:** | 17 litres (3.7 gall). |
| **Dry weight:** | 165kg (374 lb). Without screen and panniers (standard on UK models). |
| **Max speed:** | 104 mph. |
| **UK price:** | £4699. |

Also available is the V35 Florida (not imported into UK).

## 750 Targa

| | |
|---|---|
| **Engine:** | 743.9cc 90-degree V-twin ohv. |
| **Bore stoke:** | 80×74mm. |
| **Compression ratio:** | 9.7:1. |
| **Transmission:** | primary by helical gears, secondary by cardan shaft and bevel gears. |
| **Clutch:** | single disc, dry-type. |
| **Fuel delivery:** | 2 Dell'Orto PHBH 30 carburettors. |
| **Electrical system:** | 12-volt, alternator 14V-20A, rectifier and regulator. 20 amp hour battery. |
| **Starting:** | electric. |
| **Ignition:** | electronic, magnetic pick-up. |
| **Gearbox:** | 5-speed. |
| **Brakes:** | front, twin 270mm disc; rear, single 235mm disc. |
| **Wheels:** | cast alloy 18 in F and R. |
| **Instrument panel:** | speedometer, tachometer and warning lights. |
| **Fuel tank capacity:** | 18 litres (3.9 gall). |
| **Dry weight:** | 180kg (396 lb). |
| **Max speed:** | 116 mph. |
| **UK price:** | £4799. |

# 750 NTX

**Engine:** 743.9cc 90-degree V-twin ohv.

**Bore stoke:** 80×74mm.

**Compression ratio:** 9.7:1.

**Transmission:** primary by helical gears, secondary by cardan shaft and bevel gears.

**Clutch:** single disc, dry-type.

**Fuel delivery:** 2 Dell'Orto PHBH 30 carburettors.

**Electrical system:** 12-volt, alternator 14V-20A, rectifier and regulator. 24 amp hour battery.

**Starting:** electric.

**Ignition:** electronic, magnetic pick-up.

**Gearbox:** 5-speed.

**Brakes:** front, single 260mm disc (with 4-piston caliper); rear, single 260mm disc.

**Wheels:** spoked wire with alloy rims 21 in F, 18 in R.

**Instrument panel:** speedometer, tachometer and warning lights.

**Fuel tank capacity:** 30 litres (6.6 gall).

**Dry weight:** 180kg (396 lb).

**Max speed:** 106 mph.

**UK price:** Not imported.

## 750 SP

| | | | |
|---|---|---|---|
| **Engine:** | 743.9cc 90-degree V-twin ohv. | **Gearbox:** | 5-speed. |
| **Bore stoke:** | 80×74mm. | **Brakes:** | front, twin 270mm disc; rear, single 235mm disc. |
| **Compression ratio:** | 9.7:1. | **Wheels:** | cast alloy 18 in F and R. |
| **Transmission:** | primary by helical gears, secondary by cardan shaft and bevel gears. | **Instrument panel:** | speedometer, tachometer quartz clock, voltmeter and warning lights. |
| **Clutch:** | single disc, dry-type. | **Fuel tank capacity:** | 17 litres (3.7 gall). |
| **Fuel delivery:** | 2 Dell'Orto PHBH 30 carburettors. | **Dry weight:** | 185kg (408 lb). |
| **Electrical system:** | 12-volt, alternator 14V-20A, rectifier and regulator. 24 amp hour battery. | **Max speed:** | 106 mph. |
| | | **UK price:** | £5299. |
| **Starting:** | electric. | | |
| **Ignition:** | electronic, magnetic pick-up. | | |

This model is also available as the 750T, a basic touring version, without fairing, panniers, etc. at £4299.

# 750 Nevada

| | |
|---|---|
| **Engine:** | 743.9cc 90-degree V-twin ohv. |
| **Bore stoke:** | 80×74mm. |
| **Compression ratio:** | 9.7:1. |
| **Transmission:** | primary by helical gears, secondary by cardan shaft and bevel gears. |
| **Clutch:** | single disc, dry-type. |
| **Fuel delivery:** | 2 Dell'Orto PHBH 30 carburettors. |
| **Electrical system:** | 12-volt, alternator 14V-20A, rectifier and regulator. 24 amp hour battery. |
| **Starting:** | electric. |
| **Ignition:** | electronic, magnetic pick-up. |
| **Gearbox:** | 5-speed. |
| **Brakes:** | front, twin 270mm discs; rear, single 260mm disc. |
| **Wheels:** | spoked wire with alloy rims, 18 in F, 16 in R. |
| **Instrument panel:** | speedometer, tachometer and warning lights. |
| **Fuel tank capacity:** | 17 litres (3.7 gall). |
| **Dry weight:** | 177kg (389 lb). |
| **Max speed:** | 106 mph. |
| **UK price:** | £4999. |

# Mille GT

**Engine:** 948.8cc 90-degree V-twin ohv.

**Bore stoke:** 88×78mm.

**Compression ratio:** 9.2:1.

**Transmission:** primary by helical gears, secondary by cardan shaft and bevel gears.

**Clutch:** double disc, dry-type.

**Fuel delivery:** 2 Dell'Orto PHF 30 carburettors.

**Electrical system:** 12-volt, alternator 280VA. 24 amp hour battery.

**Starting:** electric.

**Ignition:** distributor.

**Gearbox:** 5-speed.

**Brakes:** front, twin 300mm disc; rear, single 242mm disc.

**Wheels:** cast alloy, 18 in F and R.

**Instrument panel:** speedometer, tachometer and warning lights.

**Fuel tank capacity:** 22.5 litres (4.9 gall).

**Dry weight:** 250kg (550 lb).

**Max speed:** 120 mph.

**UK price:** £5199 with cast wheels; £5299 with spoked wheels.

# 1000 SP III

| | |
|---|---|
| **Engine:** | 948.8cc 90-degree V-twin ohv. |
| **Bore stoke:** | 88×78mm. |
| **Compression ratio:** | 9.5:1. |
| **Transmission:** | primary by helical gears, secondary by cardan shaft and bevel gears. |
| **Clutch:** | double disc, dry-type. |
| **Fuel delivery:** | 2 Dell'Orto PHF 36 carburettors. |
| **Electrical system:** | 12-volt, alternator 14V-20A, rectifier and regulator. 24 amp hour battery. |
| **Starting:** | electric. |

| | |
|---|---|
| **Ignition:** | electronic, magnetic pick-up. |
| **Gearbox:** | 5-speed. |
| **Brakes:** | front, twin 300mm disc; rear, single 270mm disc. |
| **Wheels:** | cast alloy 18 in F and R. |
| **Instrument panel:** | speedometer, tachometer, voltmeter and warning lights. |
| **Fuel tank capacity:** | 22.5 litres (4.9 gall). |
| **Dry weight:** | 230kg (506 lb). |
| **Max speed:** | 122 mph. |
| **UK price:** | £5999. |

# Le Mans 1000

**Engine:** 948.8cc 90-degree V-twin ohv.

**Bore stoke:** 88×78mm.

**Compression ratio:** 10:1.

**Transmission:** primary by helical gears, secondary by cardan shaft and bevel gears.

**Clutch:** double disc, dry-type.

**Fuel delivery:** 2 Dell'Orto PHM 40 with accelerator pumps.

**Electrical system:** 12-volt, alternator 14V-20A, rectifier and regulator. 24 amp hour battery.

**Starting:** electric.

**Ignition:** distributor.

**Gearbox:** 5-speed.

**Brakes:** front, twin 270mm disc; rear, single 270mm disc.

**Wheels:** cast alloy 18 in F and R.

**Instrument panel:** speedometer, tachometer, voltmeter and warning lights.

**Fuel tank capacity:** 25 litres (5.5 gall).

**Dry weight:** 215kg (473 lb).

**Max speed:** 143 mph.

**UK price:** £6199.

# 1000 California (Carburettors)

**Engine:** 948.8cc 90-degree V-twin ohv.

**Bore stoke:** 88×78mm.

**Compression ratio:** 9.2:1.

**Transmission:** primary by helical gears, secondary by cardan shaft and bevel gears.

**Clutch:** double disc, dry-type.

**Fuel delivery:** 2 Dell'Orto PHF 30 carburettors.

**Electrical system:** 12-volt, alternator 14V-20A, 24 amp hour battery.

**Starting:** electric.

**Ignition:** distributor.

**Gearbox:** 5-speed.

**Brakes:** front, twin 300mm disc; rear, single 270mm disc.

**Wheels:** cast alloy 18 in F and R.

**Instrument panel:** speedometer, tachometer, voltmeter, quartz clock and warning lights.

**Fuel tank capacity:** 25 litres (5.5 gall).

**Dry weight:** 270kg (595 lb).

**Max speed:** 114 mph.

**UK price:** LAPD model £6649; FF (Fully Faired) £7399. Spoked wheels £150 extra. Also California Classic without accessories, spoked wheels as standard, £5999.

# 1000 California (Injection)

**Engine:** 948.8cc 90-degree V-twin ohv.

**Bore stoke:** 88×78mm.

**Compression ratio:** 9.2:1.

**Transmission:** primary by helical gears, secondary by cardan shaft and bevel gears.

**Clutch:** double disc, dry-type.

**Fuel delivery:** digital electronic injection Weber IAW ALFA-N system with electric feeding pump.

**Electrical system:** 12-volt, alternator 14V-20A. 24 amp hour battery.

**Starting:** electric.

**Ignition:** digital computerized electronic Weber IAW system, inductive spark.

**Gearbox:** 5-speed.

**Brakes:** front, twin 300mm disc; rear, single 270mm disc.

**Wheels:** cast alloy 18 in F and R.

**Instrument panel:** speedometer, electronic tachometer, quartz clock, check-system and warning lights.

**Fuel tank capacity:** 25 litres (5.5 gall).

**Dry weight:** 279kg (615 lb).

**Max speed:** 119 mph.

**UK price:** LAPD £7399; FF (Fully Faired) £7799. Spoked wheels £150 extra.

# 1000 S and SE

**Engine:** 948.8cc 90-degree V-twin ohv.

**Bore stoke:** 88×78mm.

**Compression ratio:** 10:1.

**Transmission:** primary by helical gears, secondary by cardan shaft and bevel gears.

**Clutch:** double disc, dry-type.

**Fuel delivery:** 2 Dell'Orto PHM 40 with accelerator pumps.

**Electrical system:** 12-volt, alternator 14V-20A. 24 amp hour battery.

**Starting:** electric.

**Ignition:** distributor.

**Gearbox:** 5-speed.

**Brakes:** front, twin 270mm disc; rear, single 270mm disc.

**Wheels:** cast alloy or spoked with alloy rims 18 in F and R.

**Instrument panel:** speedometer, tachometer and warning lights.

**Fuel tank capacity:** 24 litres (5.3 gall).

**Dry weight:** 215kg (473 lb), 1000 S; 218kg (480 lb), 1000 SE.

**Max speed:** 137 mph.

**UK price:** 1000 S £6299, 1000 SE £5999.* 1000 SE has handlebar fairing.

# 1000 Quota

**Engine:** 948.8cc 90-degree V-twin ohv.

**Bore stoke:** 88×78mm.

**Compression ratio:** 9.5:1.

**Transmission:** primary by helical gears, secondary by cardan shaft and bevel gears.

**Clutch:** double disc, dry-type.

**Fuel delivery:** Weber twin choke 36mm.

**Electrical system:** 12-volt, alternator 14V-20A. 20 amp hour battery.

**Starting:** electric.

**Ignition:** electronic, Motoplat dual pick-up.

**Gearbox:** 5-speed.

**Brakes:** front, single 300mm disc; rear, single 260mm disc.

**Wheels:** spoked with alloy rims 21 in F, 17 in R.

**Instrument panel:** speedometer, tachometer and warning lights.

**Fuel tank capacity:** 22 litres (4.8 gall).

**Dry weight:** 210kg (460 lb).

**Max speed:** 125 mph.

**UK price:** not imported.

# 1000 Daytona

**Engine:** 992cc 90-degree V-twin ohv.

**Bore stoke:** 90×78mm.

**Compression ratio:** 10:1.

**Transmission:** primary by helical gears, secondary by cardan shaft with double universal joint, bevel gears and floating housing.

**Clutch:** double disc, dry-type.

**Fuel delivery:** Weber Marelli electronic injection with dual injectors, electric feeding pump and digital optimized control of injection times.

**Electrical system:** 12-volt, alternator 14V-20A. 24 amp hour battery.

**Starting:** electric.

**Ignition:** electronic Weber Marelli digital electronic, inductive spark ALFA-N system.

**Gearbox:** 5-speed.

**Brakes:** front, twin 300mm disc; rear, single 275mm disc.

**Wheels:** cast alloy 17 in F and 18 in R.

**Instrument panel:** speedometer, tachometer and warning lights.

**Fuel tank capacity:** 25 litres (5.5 gall).

**Dry weight:** 205kg (447 lb).

**Max speed:** 153 mph.

**UK price:** to be announced.

*CHAPTER 16*

# Owners'
# Club

Today the marque owners' club is more popular than ever and Moto Guzzi owners worldwide have displayed their interest in belonging to some sort of organization where they can meet other enthusiasts with like-minded interests.

The British Guzzi organization is the Moto Guzzi Club GB. Formed in 1975 by Ed Long and Mike Carter it currently boasts around 1000 members, 10 per cent of whom live abroad, mainly in the old British Commonwealth countries of Australia, New Zealand and Canada, plus the USA. There are also a number of members in France.

One of the Honorary Life members is the famous Irishman Stanley Woods, who gained so much success for the Italian company in the 1930s.

The Club's magazine, *Gambalunga*, is published quarterly, whilst the leading event of the year is the V-twin Rally. Now in its 15th year, it is held over the August Bank Holiday weekend at The Cricket Field, Shaftesbury, Dorset. Not just a Guzzi event, owners of any make/model of V-twin are welcome — even those who ride Japanese versions.

The current membership fee for the Moto Guzzi Club GB is £12.50. Besides its journal and the various events staged throughout the year, the Club also runs a basic spares scheme. This centres around quick-moving service items and includes Venhill cables and Ferodo brake pads, at considerable savings over normal retail prices.

Moto Guzzi owners in the United States have a well organized and active club, the Moto Guzzi National Owner's Club, run by Frank Wedge. The MGNOC publishes a monthly newsletter and holds many national and local rallies every year, Membership costs $23 per year.

Obviously, whether or not you join a club is a very personal thing. But a big plus for being a member is that it brings you into contact with like minded enthusiasts.

**Useful addresses**

**Moto Guzzi Owners' Club GB**
Simon Howers
The General Secretary
106 The Chase
Wallington
Surrey
SM6 8LY
Great Britain

**Moto Guzzi, National Owners' Club**
Frank Wedge
PO Box 98
Olmitz
Kansas 67564
USA

# CHAPTER 17

# Bibliography

**Ayton, Cyril.** *Guide to Italian Motorcyles*
Temple Press, 1985, 156 pages.
ISBN NO. 0-600-35141-6.

Small pocket-size book covering a selection of models from the major Italian motorcycle manufacturers; 28 pages dealing with the following Guzzi models: Sport 14, Zigolo, Lodola 175, V8 racer, V1000, Le Mans and Spada.

**Columbo, Mario.** *Moto Guzzi*
Milan, 1977. 384 pages.

Large-format Italian language history of Guzzi motorcycles, racing and production. Updated 1983, and to be published in English during 1991 with 413 pages and over 500 illustrations. Highly acclaimed, although expensive. Also lists useful frame numbers for standard production models.

**Columbo, Mario.** *Moto Guzzi Genius and Sport*
Automobilia, 1983. 128 pages.
ISBN No. 88-85058-33-7.

Small, brief, hard-covered history of the company. Liberally illustrated, with some colour.

**Darlington, Mansur.**
*Moto Guzzi 750, 850 & 1000*
*V-twins Workshop Manual*
Haynes Publishing Group, 1979. 158 pages.
ISBN No. 0-85696-339-9.

Affordable, if not perfect. Reasonable coverage, but hampered by covering only the earlier models.

**Nutting, John.** *Superbikes of the Seventies*
Hamlyn, 1978. 128 pages. ISBN No. 0600-38222-2.

Essentially *Superbikes of the Seventies* is based on road tests originally published by the British weekly, *Motor Cycle*. Although the Le Mans I is the only Guzzi included, it provides good coverage of its main competitors during the 1970s.

**Parker, Tim.** *Italian Motorcycles—Classic Sports Bikes*
Osprey Publishing, 1984. 128 pages.
ISBN No. 0-85045-576-6.

A softback book in the Osprey colour series. It features eight of the main Italian marques (including, of course, Moto Guzzi). The Mandello del Lario marque gets 22 pages and some of the best pictures in the entire book are in the Guzzi section, including a Nuovo Falcone, 850 Eldorado, various Califo nias, V7 Sport, Le Mans I, II and III, plus several of the smaller vees. A coffee table offering, rather than any real depth, but a definite plus is the colourful photography.

**Renstrom, Richard.** *Great Motorcycle Legends*
Haessner Publishing Inc., 1977. 128 pages.
ISBN No. 0-87880-011-5.

A revised version of the book by the same author entitled *The Great Motorcycles*, this contains a chapter dealing with Guzzi's history (most of it about the racing exploits) until the late 1960s. Compared to Mario Columbo's later book, this is really basic stuff.

**Rivola, Luigi.** *Racing Motorcycles*
Galley Press, 1977. 320 pages.

Although it only deals with the racing side of the company, and then only certain individual machines, it's still worth getting as there are some lovely colour illustrations. Machines covered: 500 Four-valve 1924, 250 Single-shaft 1930, 500 In-line four 1953, 500 V-twin 1951, 250 Gambalunghino 1952, 350 Single-shaft 1953, 350 Two-shaft 1956 and 500 V8 1956.

**Scott, Michael & Cutts, John.**
*The World's Fastest Motorcycles*
The Apple Press, 1987. 128 pages.
ISBN No. 1-85076-067-5.

Only one Guzzi featured, the Le Mans 1000 – although photographs show a Mark I and Mark III – both of which are 850s. Nicely produced big-format book, but lacking any real information.

**Walker, Mick.** *Moto Guzzi Twins*
Osprey Publishing, 1986. 192 pages.
ISBN No. 0-85045-650-9.

A history of all the post-war twins. Whilst it concentrates mainly on the V-twin models, it also covers the parallel twins in both their two and four-stroke guises. Final chapter deals with Alejandro de Tomaso's career and his influence on events since taking over Moto Guzzi in late 1972. Appendices contain specifications, colours, carburettor settings, prices, and model recognition.

**Walker, Mick.** *Moto Guzzi Singles*
Osprey Publishing, 1986. 192 pages.
ISBN No. 0-85045-712-2.

Covers roadsters, racers and even the marque's ISDT bikes. Starts with the founding fathers – Guzzi and Parodi – and ends with the de Tomaso era. Airone, Falcone, Galletto, Lodola and Stornello; these and many others are covered, together with both factory and privateer racing efforts. Has the same detailed appendices as the *Twins* volume above.

**Walker, Mick.** *Italian Classic Gallery–*
*The Racing Bikes*
Haynes Publishing Group, 1991. 192 pages.

Large-format book with over 330 monochrome and colour photographs from author's personal collection giving a unique view of the men, machines and atmosphere of the post-war classic era of Italian racing motorcycles. Large Moto Guzzi section.

**Walker, Mick.** *Italian Classic Gallery–*
*The Road Bikes*
Haynes Publishing Group, 1991. 192 pages.

Companion volume to the above.

**Walker, Mick.** *Italian Motorcycles*
Aston Publications, 1991. 240 pages.

Detailed descriptions and development histories of all the famous – and not so famous – Italian marques. Moto Guzzi is particularly well covered. 200,000 words, 200 black and white photographs plus eight pages of colour. A total of well over 200 individual marques are covered.

# CHAPTER 18

# Sources of Parts

Although it might appear easier to deal with your friendly dealer, my advice is don't. For a start it is unlikely that he will stock very much in the way of parts which will fit Moto Guzzis and even if he does have the odd oil filter or clutch cable for a V50, it's highly unlikely that he will have anything much for old models.

Another point, from personal experience, is that it takes several years for someone to become knowledgeable enough in Moto Guzzis to be able to do the job properly, however much that person may wish to please.

Knowing what fits where on a particular model takes time, so for once experience

Besides Moto Guzzi themselves, several other companies manufacture 'original' parts for the Italian marque.

does count for something.

To Guzzi's credit they have established a major modern parts warehouse complex in Modena from where distribution to both domestic and export markets is effected. This if for all 'modern' models such as V-twins, the post 1970 two-strokes and all other models manufactured since the de Tomaso takeover in 1972.

As for earlier bikes such as the horizontal four-stroke singles, the Galletto and the Zigolo two-stroke, the entire stockholding of parts was sold off to a specialist Italian dealer, Marco Ferrari, M Ferrari & C, Corso della Vittoria 65, Novara, Italy. Some other Italian dealers also stock some parts for these obsolete machines.

Besides new items, there is the question of used parts. Provided these are serviceable they can often not only solve a problem if a new item is not available, but will also be cheaper (or should be). Recently, with the price of complete machines of the classic era rising rapidly, far fewer older motorcycles have been broken for parts and this process is likely to continue, so making used parts more difficult to find.

Two members of the Lafranconi silencer factory's senior management with one of their products for a 1950s Guzzi single, seen in November 1988.

An aftermarket air filter such as this can improve performance on a number of models, including this SP1000.

One of several frame kits for the large-capacity Guzzi vees. This monoshock example was seen at the Milan Show in November 1987. Note also the performance exhaust systems, rear sets, clip-ons and oil-cooler kit.

Therefore, on the surface both new and used Guzzi spares would seem to be rather difficult to find. Happily, at least to date, this has not proved to be the case in practice. This is mainly due to certain specialist dealers carrying comprehensive stocks of parts. This means that, provided you deal with these specialists you should not experience too many problems – and besides their large stocks, these specialists will often be able to answer technical queries.

As for the bits which prove more difficult to locate, larger cycle parts like tanks, seats, side panels and mudguards are most obviously at risk thanks to there often being more than one colour scheme and also their vulnerability to damage when in storage. These two factors alone often deter dealers from stocking these particular items. Traditionally engine bits have been the easiest to find, but obviously each model has its own particular difficult areas.

My advice is if your normal supplier cannot come up with the part you need try someone else, for he might just have that elusive component tucked away somewhere. Also remember the world is growing smaller through more efficient communications – try a foreign supplier if necessary.

Finally there are autojumbles, or you could even resort to advertising... but in any case don't give up.

## British sources – Moto Guzzi parts

**Spares GB,** 1 Walpole Road, Colliers Wood, London SW19 2BZ

**Moto Cinelli,** Unit 1, Tyne Road, Weedon Road Industrial Estate, Northampton NN5 5AF

**Moto Mania,** Unit 148, Deptford Market, Deptford, London

**Italsport,** 8-14 Chester Road, Manchester M15 4NT

**Rotadale,** 34 Selhurst Road, London SE25

**Moto Mecca Spares Ltd,** Unit 302, Woolsbridge Industrial Park, Old Barn Farm Road, Three Legged Cross, Wimborne, Dorset BH21 6SP

## American sources – Moto Guzzi parts

**Arlette,** 111 North Bell, Cedar Park, Texas 78613

**Eish Enterprises,** 11041 Opel Road NE, Salineville, Ohio 43945

**Raceco Cycles,** 333 Kent Avenue, Brooklyn, New York 11211

**Fred Heistand Motors,** 734 Conestagna Avenue, Manheim, PA

**Dale's Cycle,** 2401-3 Avenue, Pock Island, Illinois 61201

**Ronco Cycles,** 15621 East 21st Street, Wichita, Kansas 67230

**Moto Guzzi Classics**, 2370 Walnut Avenue, Signal Hill, CA 90806

**Harper's Moto Guzzi,** 32401 Stringtown Road, Greenwood, M0 64034

**Midway Cycles,** Lillington, North Carolina

# CHAPTER 19

# Used Bike Market

Whatever the star rating and however much you would like to own the model of your choice, there is one vital factor: money!

Buying secondhand gives you much more flexibility in this area, or at least it should.

Before you even start you must have your finances fully sorted. This includes how much you are going to limit your spending to, and how you are going to borrow the money if it's not sitting in your bank account. With credit, obviously shop around for the very best possible deal.

Once the sordid business of financial matters is over you can begin looking seriously. Where you look first is really governed by which country you reside in and which model you have set your heart on.

The best buys, or in other words value for money, are usually the machines which do not reach the stage of being advertised. But conversely these are the most difficult to find if you are looking for an exact model and will not be satisfied with anything else.

The annoying thing is for all you know just the bike you want may well be sitting in someone's lock-up garage hidden from view to the world, and with it's owner wanting to sell, but not knowing how to go about it, or just too lazy to actually advertise it, just around the corner!

The following are the more accepted ways of finding a used bike:

1 Local newspaper – in the classified section.
2 Local dealer
3 Specialist motorcycle press classifieds
4 Specialist dealer
5 For older machines – autojumbles and the like

What you have to bear in mind is that a machine purchased privately will not normally be covered by any form of warranty, whereas one from a dealer will be subject to the various trading standards laws of each particular country. Even so, with careful and intelligent work it *is* possible to make some excellent buys privately, and most Moto Guzzi owners are genuine enthusiasts themselves, so you are less likely to be offered a 'rogue' without knowing it. But even so, don't *assume* that everything is right; check it or take someone along who has the necessary technical expertise.

There are obviously other ways of finding the right bike, through race meetings, club magazines, rallies or even other owners.

If all else fails why not try placing an ad yourself? Probably the best method is to use any of the specialist magazines that operate free classifieds for their readers. Normally these are monthlies, so this will require waiting a few weeks. For 'instant' results you will have to use something which appears weekly (*Motor Cycle News*, for example, in

Guzzi enthusiast and dealer Vincent Marcello of London Italian specialists Rotadale (right) with a couple of customers discussing a secondhand V50 (centre).

A section of the Mick Walker Motorcycles' Wisbech showroom in the mid-1970s, with a line-up of several Guzzis to the left of the photograph. Included are the 125 Turismo, 750 S3, V1000 Convert, 850T and Le Mans I.

Britain), but then you will have to pay.

Finally if you are purchasing an older machine which carries the classic tag, make sure your insurance cover is on an agreed value basis. Many insurance companies now operate a scheme where an older motorcycle can be covered in this way. It will certainly save you a lot of heartache, not to say financial loss, if your pride and joy is later damaged or stolen.

To give British and American readers a guide, there follows a list of the specialist magazines which are the best bet to find a Moto Guzzi advertised, or to place a wanted advertisement yourself.

# USEFUL NAMES AND ADDRESSES:

**Great Britain**
**Motor Cycle News,** 20-22 Station Rd, Kettering, Northants NN15 7HH
**Classic Bike,** EMAP National Publications Bushfield House, Orton Centre Peterborough PE2 0UW
**The Classic Motorcycle** (as for Classic Bike)
**Motorcycle Sport,** Standard House, Bonhill Street, London, EC2A 4DA
**Classic Motorcycling Legends,** 80 Kingsway East, Dundee, DD4 8SL
**Motorcycle International,** PO Box 707, London SW4 7UE

**USA**
**Cycle World,** 1499 Monrovia Ave, Newport Beach, CA 92663
**Motorcyclist** PO Box 3296, Los Angeles, CA 90078
**Cycle News** PO Box 498, Long Beach, CA 90801-0498
**Motorcyclist's Post** PO Box 154, Rochdale, MA 01542
**Walnick's Classic 'Fieds,** 8280 Janes Avenue, Woodridge, IL 60517